Eating Disord

This book presents an accessible introduction to the conceptualization and treatment of eating disorders from a psychoanalytic perspective.

Each of the chapters offers a different perspective on these difficult-to-treat conditions and, taken together, illustrates the breadth and depth that psychoanalytic thinking can offer both seasoned clinicians and those just beginning to explore the field. Different aspects of how psychoanalytic theory and practice can engage with eating disorders are addressed, including mobilizing its nuanced developmental theories to illustrate the difficulties these patients have with putting feelings into words, the loathing that they feel toward their bodies, the disharmonies they experience in the link between body and mind, and even the ways that they engage with online Internet forums.

This is an accessible read for clinicians at the start of their career and will also be a useful, novel take on the subject for experienced practitioners.

Tom Wooldridge is an associate professor of psychology, psychoanalyst, and board-certified, licensed psychologist. He has published numerous journal articles on a range of topics as well as several books.

Routledge Introductions to
Contemporary Psychoanalysis
Aner Govrin, Ph.D. Series Editor
Tair Caspi, Ph.D. Associate Editor

"Routledge Introductions to Contemporary Psychoanalysis" is one of the prominent psychoanalytic publishing ventures of our day. It will comprise dozens of books that will serve as concise introductions dedicated to influential concepts, theories, leading figures, and techniques in psychoanalysis covering every important aspect of psychoanalysis.

The length of each book is fixed at 40,000 words.

The series' books are designed to be easily accessible so as to provide informative answers in various areas of psychoanalytic thought. Each book will provide updated ideas on topics relevant to contemporary psychoanalysis – from the unconscious and dreams, projective identification and eating disorders, through neuropsychoanalysis, colonialism and spiritual-sensitive psychoanalysis. Books will also be dedicated to prominent figures in the field, such as Melanie Klein, Jaque Lacan, Sandor Ferenczi, Otto Kernberg and Michael Eigen.

Not serving solely as an introduction for beginners, the purpose of the series is to offer compendiums of information on particular topics within different psychoanalytic schools. We not only ask authors to review a topic but also address the readers with their own personal views and contribution to the specific chosen field. Books will make intricate ideas comprehensible without compromising their complexity.

We aim to make contemporary psychoanalysis more accessible to both clinicians and the general educated public.

Donald Meltzer: A Contemporary Introduction
Meg Harris Williams

For more information on this series, please visit: www.routledge.com/ Routledge-Literature-Companions/book-series/RC4444

Eating Disorders

A Contemporary Introduction

Tom Wooldridge

Routledge
Taylor & Francis Group

LONDON AND NEW YORK

Cover image: © Michal Heiman, *Asylum 1855–2020, The Sleeper* (video, psychoanalytic sofa and Plate 34), exhibition view, Herzliya Museum of Contemporary Art, 2017

First published 2023
by Routledge
4 Park Square, Milton Park, Abingdon, Oxon OX14 4RN

and by Routledge
605 Third Avenue, New York, NY 10158

Routledge is an imprint of the Taylor & Francis Group, an informa business

© 2023 Tom Wooldridge

British Library Cataloguing-in-Publication Data
A catalogue record for this book is available from the British Library

Library of Congress Cataloging-in-Publication Data
Names: Wooldridge, Tom, author.
Title: Eating disorders : a contemporary introduction / Tom Wooldridge.
Description: Abingdon, Oxon ; New York, NY : Routledge, 2023. | Series: Routledge introductions to contemporary psychoanalysis | Includes bibliographical references and index.
Identifiers: LCCN 2022010347 | ISBN 9780367861209 (hardback) | ISBN 9780367861216 (paperback) | ISBN 9781003016991 (ebook)
Subjects: LCSH: Eating disorders.
Classification: LCC RC552.E18 W65 2023 | DDC 616.85/26—dc23/eng/20220330
LC record available at https://lccn.loc.gov/2022010347

ISBN: 978-0-367-86120-9 (hbk)
ISBN: 978-0-367-86121-6 (pbk)
ISBN: 978-1-003-01699-1 (ebk)

DOI: 10.4324/9781003016991

Typeset in Times New Roman
by Apex CoVantage, LLC

Contents

Introduction

This book is intended to introduce students and clinicians as well as general readers to the psychoanalytic conceptualization and treatment of eating disorders. Each of the nine chapters offers a different perspective on these difficult-to-treat syndromes and, taken together, illustrates the breadth and depth that psychoanalytic thinking can offer both seasoned clinicians and those just beginning to explore the field. Because this volume does not aim to be comprehensive, each chapter is chosen to specifically illustrate different aspects of how psychoanalytic theory and practice can engage with eating disorders, including mobilizing its nuanced developmental theories to illustrate the difficulties these patients have with putting feelings into words, the loathing that they feel toward their bodies, the disharmonies they experience in the link between body and mind, and even the ways that they engage with online Internet forums.

But at the outset, it must be acknowledged that the term *eating disorders* refers to a set of descriptive diagnoses – anorexia nervosa, bulimia nervosa, binge-eating disorder, muscle dysmorphia, orthorexia, to name those most recognized – that describe sets of observable symptoms and behavioral phenomena. This stands in contrast to psychodynamic or structural diagnoses, which emphasize the patient's personality structure, including its underlying psychodynamic mechanisms, to understand her as a whole person. Because eating disorders are descriptive diagnoses, they do not point to homogenous groups of people but, instead, group together people who have similar observable symptoms and behaviors.

DOI: 10.4324/9781003016991-1

To illustrate this point, consider an empirical study that uses the Shedler-Westen Assessment Protocol (SWAP-200) to assess the personality structure of patients with anorexia nervosa and bulimia nervosa. Three categories of patients emerge: a high-functioning/ perfectionistic group, a constricted/overcontrolled group, and an emotionally dysregulated/undercontrolled group. As this study suggests, reliance on descriptive diagnosis groups together anorexic patients who are high-functioning and self-critical with those who are highly disturbed, constricted, and avoidant, while also grouping together bulimic patients who are high functioning and self-critical with those who are highly disturbed, impulsive, and emotionally dysregulated (Westen & Harnden-Fischer, 2001). For the purposes of this book, "eating disorders" refers to a heterogenous group of people who, despite their underlying differences, all struggle with difficulties in relation to food, weight, and body shape. Distinctions such as those in the aforementioned study are profoundly clinically relevant yet lost with sole reliance upon descriptive diagnosis. Psychoanalytic thinking is of immense value to clinicians working with eating disorders for its ability to clarify such distinctions and to elaborate on their treatment implications.

With this point in mind, each chapter in this volume is chosen because it offers a way of thinking that will be applicable to a wide range – though certainly not all – patients with eating disorders encountered in clinical practice. Although clinical practice with this population, especially with patients at medical risk, demands extensive training and supervision, this book is intended to provide an introduction. It is hoped that it will be useful for psychoanalytically trained clinicians and students who are working with patients with eating disorders and for generalist clinicians who are interested in learning more about what psychoanalytic thinking can offer.

This book is intended to fill an important gap in the literature. Despite the long history of psychoanalytic work on eating disorders, contemporary endeavors have lost sight of the insights our field has provided. Most practitioners who work with eating disorders focus on so-called "evidence-based treatments" that emphasize rapid symptom reduction and neglect underlying psychodynamic structure. For example, the "gold standard" treatment for adolescents with anorexia nervosa is family-based therapy, which promotes an "agnostic" position with regard to etiological factors, particularly the family's role in the child's developing an eating disorder (Lock, Le Grange, Agras, & Dare, 2001). This position can be effective in mitigating shame and stigma, which facilitates treatment engagement – a first step with a population that is often difficult to engage in treatment. In my own practice, I refer patients to FBT treatments to facilitate weight restoration and as a steppingstone to engagement with deeper treatment. Yet I am also always aware that an emphasis on rapid symptom reduction may also lead us to neglect less overt, and less easily measurable, aspects of the patient's experience. Patients with eating disorders contend with an emotional landscape marked by isolation and loneliness as well as shame, guilt, and embarrassment, not to mention a profound hopelessness about the possibilities of emotional connection. Help with these struggles will never be found in a pill or a set of therapeutic exercises, in spite of the potential usefulness of both. It is only through a meaningful emotional connection that we can help patients begin to "bear the unbearable and to say the unsayable" (Atwood, 2012, p. 118).

In a field in which manualized, symptom-focused treatments are increasingly deployed in clinical practice, psychoanalysis provides a refreshing counterpoint with its emphasis on the depth and complexity of the individual. Especially when combined with other modalities such as nutritional rehabilitation, psychopharmacology, and developmental help, as well as an in-depth knowledge of the interaction between psychodynamics and sociocultural phenomena,[1] it provides a uniquely powerful means of assisting patients struggling with these complex, even deadly, clinical syndromes. Analysts who work with eating and body image problems often hear stories about the crushing impact of multigenerational criticism about weight, body type, and appearance (Zerbe, 2016). We hear, too, about the multiple meanings of food, weight, and body shape and how those meanings are embedded in complex familial and cultural systems. Throughout all of this, we attempt to understand and resonate with the deep anguish conveyed by bodily sufferings. Reflecting on this difficult work, I have often thought that our emphasis on rapid symptom reduction signifies not only our intent to help as quickly as possible but also our need to evade confrontation with our patients' profound emotional pain (and perhaps, at times, our own).

From a psychoanalytic point of view, full recovery from an eating disorder is tantamount to the growth and development of the personality. Ernest Becker (1964) captures the extent of the change required for full recovery quite eloquently, so I will quote him in full.

> The patient is not struggling against himself, against forces deep within his animal nature. He is struggling rather against the loss of his world, of the whole range of action and objects that he so laboriously fashioned during his early training. He is fighting, in sum, against the subversion of himself in the only world that he knows. Each object is as much a part of him as is the built-in behavior pattern for transacting with the object. Each action is as much within his nature as the feeling he derives from initiating or contemplating that action. Each rule for behavior is as much part of him as his metabolism, the forward momentum of his life processes . . . the rules, objects, and self-feeling are fused – taken together they constitute one's "world." How is one to relinquish his world unless he first gains a new one? This is the basic problem of personality change (pp. 170–179).

Overview of the Book

In *Chapter 1: Alexithymia and the Psychic Elaboration of Emotion*, we will discuss the difficulty that many patients with eating disorders have putting feelings into words. Some patients may struggle to describe and elaborate on their experience, for instance, of need, desire, or hunger. While they can speak to their feelings, often quite articulately, in other realms, in these particular areas this capacity is conspicuously absent. Other patients' difficulties manifest more globally, as trouble putting feelings into words that extend across most or all domains. The capacity to think about, to reflect upon, difficult feelings is what allows us to forego expressing them in more problematic ways, such as, for patients with eating disorders, through a binge, or a purge, or food restriction. With this idea in mind, we will discuss the idea of *mentalisation*, which is a way of thinking about different "registers" of emotional expression and how we can identify these in patients with eating disorders, as well as the concept of *reverie*, which speaks to the intersubjective process that occurs between parent and child as well as between clinician and patient and that is central to facilitating the capacity to identify and elaborate emotional experience.

In *Chapter 2: Early Relationships, Object Relations, and Traumatic Themes*, we discuss the contributions of object relations theory to understanding the psychological structure of patients with eating disorders. Object relations theory is concerned with how early relational experiences have been internalized as a psychological structure that continues to organize and give meaning to experiences in the present. From this point of view, it is the underlying psychological structure – not just the eating disorder symptoms that manifest because of it – that is a focus of treatment. We also discuss several traumatic themes (Shabad, 1993), or chronic patterns of frustrating and depriving childhood experience at the hands of caretakers that take on the emotional significance of cumulative trauma (Khan, 1963). These themes are chosen because they are commonly described by patients with eating disorders. Although each will only apply to some patients, these examples will clarify how underlying psychological structure, shaped by internal representations of early relationships, may manifest, symptomatically, as an eating disorder.

A central task with patients with eating disorders is facilitating the capacity to postpone action in favor of reflection, yet the pull to binge, or purge, or restrict is difficult, if not impossible, to resist. In *Chapter 3: Traumatic Themes, Repetition, and Mourning*, we begin with a discussion of Freud's (1914) notion of the compulsion to repeat and formulate the eating disordered patient's symptoms as repetitions against traumatic themes from childhood, never-ending (because never fully successful) attempts to magically undo the pain of the past (Shabad, 1993). We discuss Novick and Novick (2001, 2016) dual-track, two-systems model of development, which provides a way of thinking about the development of agency, or its curtailment, throughout life. We conclude with a discussion of mourning, which is seen as a counterpart to Freud's (1914) notion of working through. Mourning is the mechanism through which traumatic themes can be acknowledged, disillusioned wishes for an ideal object relinquished, and painful early relationships transformed into aspects of the patient's character that are carried forward in constructive ways.

Patients with eating disorders commonly describe the loathing that they experience toward their bodies. They refer to their bodies, or parts of their bodies, as disgusting, ugly, gross, and "fat." In *Chapter 4: Abjection and Bodily Disgust*, we discuss Kristeva's (1982) notion of abjection in an attempt to more fully understand this experience. We consider two traumatic themes that may contribute to the experience of abjection in these patients: a form of breakdown in containment (Williams, 1997) and the formation of a "rotten core" (Lax, 1980). In the first, the parent uses the child as a receptacle for her own unprocessed emotion, which the child experiences as a "foreign body" inserted into her vulnerable psyche. In the second, the experience of the self is split, with the rotten core representing the experience of the "bad" mother with the "bad" aspects of the self that exists alongside an experience of the self and mother as good and loveable. This traumatic theme develops in response to the mother's unavailability during separation and individuation. These ideas may facilitate our ability to empathically grasp the profound extent of the self-loathing and bodily disgust with which eating disordered patients struggle.

In *Chapter 5: Body–Mind Dissociation and False Bodies*, we explore false bodies in patients with eating disorders. The term *false body* describes how the body's state is rigidly controlled so that spontaneous emotional experiences are avoided. For some patients with binge eating disorder, the weight gain that results from eating symptoms may serve as a false body. Patients with orthorexia, who have an unhealthy focus on eating in a healthy way, may use seemingly healthy exercise regimes, including a rigidly controlled diet and obsessive self-care rituals, to maintain a false body. We will focus, however, on a particular form of the false body that is commonly observed in patients with anorexia nervosa: the entropic body (Wooldridge, 2018b). The *entropic body* is cultivated through self-starvation to subjugate an underlying emotional experience of need and dependence. It develops to compensate for the failure to internalize the caretaker's capacity to comfort and soothe the child during the period of separation and individuation. Without the capacity to provide comfort to oneself or to seek it in emotional connection with another person in hand, these patients are unable to emotionally "digest" traumatic experiences in infancy and beyond and, as a result, are forced to rely upon the entropic body to attenuate their distress.

We begin *Chapter 6: Gender, Culture, and Desire* by examining the nature of desire. From one point of view, desires are already-formed inner strivings awaiting direction. From another, desire is a function of its context, shaped in relationship and the larger cultural surround. From this perspective, the task becomes not only to uncover desires that have been defended against but also to help the patient begin to want freely so that, over time, new containers of desire can emerge. The topic of desire leads to a consideration of gender. Gender differences are dramatic in the prevalence of some eating disorders, with far more females than males diagnosed with anorexia and bulimia (Stice & Bohon, 2012). Although a cultural analysis helps to elucidate this difference, it fails to explain why females are more susceptible to certain cultural influences than their male counterparts. With this in mind, we draw upon contemporary psychoanalytic models of gender development to explore the relationship between gender identity and agency. We highlight the necessity of the developing of a diverse gender "repertoire" (Elise, 1998) – sense of oneself as both masculine and feminine in various ways – to counter problematic gender identifications.

Chapter 7: Affect Regulation, Dissociation, and Body Imaginings begins with a discussion of a perspective from the relational school of psychoanalysis that regards the self not as a unified entity but as decentralized and composed of relatively discrete psychic structures – "selves" – that, in a good enough developmental situation, attain an "illusion" of coherence and continuity (Bromberg, 1998). In this paradigm, *relational trauma* is defined as exposure to chronic misattunement and prolonged states of dysregulation in the context of an early attachment relationship. We use these ideas to formulate the notion of the "hungry self," a self-state prominent in patients with binge eating disorders. We also consider how the experience of body image may vary according to the shifting landscape of dissociatively structured self-states. We describe how body image is an expression of past relational experiences and how, in patients with histories of relational trauma, an important aspect of treatment is helping patients to "stand in the spaces" (Bromberg, 1998) to understand the dynamics driving shifting experiences of body image.

Chapter 8: The Role of the Father and the Paternal Function focuses on the role of the father and of the paternal function in patients with eating disorders, specifically on patients with anorexia nervosa and muscle dysmorphia. One purpose served by the paternal function is to assist the child in separation and individuation from his mother. A father's establishing a loving bond with his son encourages the child's capacity to explore the outside world (Abelin, 1971). In the families of a child who develops anorexia nervosa, the mother's use of the child to maintain her own equilibrium makes separation and individuation more difficult. In such families, a potentially important factor in whether the child goes on to develop anorexia nervosa is the strength of the paternal function, which optimally helps the child learn how to appropriately deploy his aggression in the service of separation and individuation. In these families, however, the relative absence of the paternal function may lead the anorexic-to-be to locate his experience of agency in relation to eating and his body, which he rigidly controls. In families of children who develop muscle dysmorphia, in contrast, the father may maintain his own equilibrium by keeping his son small, vulnerable, and weak. Whereas in optimal development the paternal function would facilitate the developing boy's separation and individuation, it instead threatens the child with the possibility of remaining forever lost in dependency upon his mother. To avoid this, the child defensively idealizes a particular form of masculinity characterized by "bigness" (Corbett, 2001) that the paternal function comes to represent and that is concretely expressed by his drive for muscularity.

In chat rooms, newsgroups, and websites, pro-anorexia has emerged in recent years as a cultural movement in cyberspace that takes an at least partially positive attitude toward anorexia nervosa and other eating disorders. Notably, there are also "pro-mia" online forums that focus on bulimia nervosa, bodybuilding websites that have many participants who struggle with muscle dysmorphia, as well as a range of other online spaces in which those struggling with food, weight, and shape interact and express themselves. In *Chapter 9: Eating Disorders in Cyberspace*, we focus specifically on how participants make psychological use of pro-anorexia websites. On the one hand, they may provide participants with a potential space (Winnicott, 1971) – a state of mind in which play and creativity are possible – that fosters psychological development, allowing them to play with ideas about relationship, identity, and even recovery. In contrast to this, they may also provide an opportunity for a psychic retreat (Steiner, 1993) in which cyberspace becomes a 'funhouse mirror' (Malater, 2007): an escape from a reality that has become unbearable and a place of "relative peace" (Steiner, 1993, p. 1). *Psychic retreats* are problematic because they foreclose the possibility of emotional growth, creativity, and authentic engagement with relationship.

Acknowledgments

I wish to thank Aner Govrin, PhD, and Tair Caspi, PhD, for inviting me to contribute this volume to their book series, *The Routledge Introductions to Contemporary Psychoanalysis*. When I received their invitation, I had been thinking about writing a book on what psychoanalysis has to offer in the treatment of eating disorders for some time, having recently edited a volume on the topic (Wooldridge, 2018a). I had hesitated to take on such a project until receiving their encouragement, for which I am deeply grateful. They have been responsive every step of the way.

I also wish to note that *Chapter 1: Alexithymia and the Psychic Elaboration of Emotion, Chapter 4: Abjection and Bodily Disgust, Chapter 5: Body–Mind Dissociation and False Bodies, Chapter 8: The Role of the Father and the Paternal*, and *Chapter 9: Eating Disorders in Cyberspace* contain material drawn from articles previously published in a peer-reviewed journal (Wooldridge, 2021b; Wooldridge, 2021b; Wooldridge, 2018b; Wooldridge, 2021a; Wooldridge, 2014). I wish to sincerely thank Gil, Jan, and Aaron at *310 Eatery* for providing me with a space to write. This book is dedicated with love and gratitude to the friends, family, and colleagues who have offered much support and affection over the years, with special mention of my son, Parker, and my parents.

Note

1 An important limitation of this book is that it does not incorporate the literature on the sociocultural factors that contribute to eating disorders or discuss interaction of these factors with the psychodynamics of individual patients. It is, unfortunately, simply not possible for me to do justice to the many important contributions that have been made in the literature, including research on the idealization of the thin body type within Western society (Bruch, 1962; Garner, Garfinkel, Schwartz, & Thompson, 1980), the role of the mass media in promoting pathogenic attitudes toward the body and self (Stice, Schupak-Neuberg, Shaw, & Stein, 1994), the promotion of dieting

behavior in athletes such as ballerinas, models, jockeys, and wrestlers (Garner & Garfinkel, 1980; Mickalide, 1990; Wooldridge, 2016; Wooldridge & Lytle, 2012), and the influence of ethnic group values upon the development and experience of eating disorders (George & Franko, 2010).

References

Abelin, E. L. (1971). The role of the father in the separation-individuation process. In B. McDevitt & C. F. Settlage (Eds.), *Separation-individuation* (pp. 229–252). New York, NY: International Universities Press.

Atwood, G. E. (2012). *The abyss of madness*. New York, NY: Taylor and Francis.

Becker, E. (1964). *The revolution in psychiatry: The new understanding of man*. New York, NY: Free Press.

Bromberg, P. M. (1998). *Standing in the spaces: Essays on clinical process, trauma, and dissociation*. Hillsdale, NJ: Analytic Press.

Bruch, H. (1962). Perceptual and conceptual disturbances in anorexia nervosa. *Psychosomatic Medicine, 24*, 187–194.

Corbett, K. (2001). Faggot = loser. *Studies in Gender & Sexuality, 2*(1), 3–28.

Elise, D. (1998). Gender repertoire: Body, mind, and bisexuality. *Psychoanalytic Dialogues, 8*(3), 353–371.

Freud, S. (1914). Remembering, repeating and working-through. *Standard Edition, 12*, 145–156.

Garner, D. M., & Garfinkel, P. E. (1980). Socio-cultural factors in the development of anorexia nervosa. *Psychological Medicine, 10*, 647–656.

Garner, D. M., Garfinkel, P. E., Schwartz, D., & Thompson, M. (1980). Cultural expectations of thinness in women. *Psychological Reports, 47*, 483–491.

George, J. B. E., & Franko, D. L. (2010). Cultural issues in eating pathology and body image among children and adolescents. *Journal of Pediatric Psychology, 35*(3), 231–242.

Khan, M. M. R. (1963). The concept of cumulative trauma. *Psychoanalytic Study of the Child, 18*, 286–306.

Kristeva, J. (1982). *Approaching abjection, powers of horror* (pp. 1–31). New York, NY: Columbia University Press.

Lax, R. (1980). The rotten core: A defect in the formation of the self during the rapprochement subphase. In R. Lax, S. Bach, & J. A. Burland (Eds.), *Rapprochement: The critical subphase of separation-individuation*. New York, NY: J. Aronson.

Lock, J., Le Grange, D., Agras, W. S., & Dare, C. (2001). *Treatment manual for anorexia nervosa: A family-based approach*. New York, NY: Guilford Press.

Malater, E. (2007). Introduction: Special issue on the internet. *The Psychoanalytic Review, 94*(1), 3–6.

Mickalide, A. D. (1990). Sociocultural factors influencing weight among males. In A. Andersen (Ed.), *Males with eating disorders* (pp. 30–39). Brunner/Mazel.

Novick, J., & Novick, K. K. (2001). Two systems of self-regulation. *Psychoanalysis and Social Work, 8*(3–4), 95–122.

Novick, J., & Novick, K. K. (2016). *Freedom to choose: Two systems of self regulation.* New York: IPBooks.

Shabad, P. (1993). Repetition and incomplete mourning: The intergenerational transmission of traumatic themes. *Psychoanalytic Psychology, 10*(1), 61–75.

Steiner, J. (1993). *Psychic retreats: Pathological organizations in psychotic, neurotic, and borderline patients.* New York, NY: Routledge.

Stice, E., & Bohon, C. (2012). Eating disorders. In T. Beauchaine & S. Lindshaw (Eds.), *Child and adolescent psychopathology* (2nd ed.). New York, NY: Wiley.

Stice, E., Schupak-Neuberg, K., Shaw, H. E., & Stein, R. I. (1994). Relation of media exposure to eating disorder symptomatology: An examination of mediating mechanisms. *Journal of Abnormal Psychology, 103*, 836–840.

Westen, D., & Harnden-Fischer, J. (2001). Personality profiles in eating disorders: Rethinking the distinction between axis I and axis II. *American Journal of Psychiatry, 158*(4), 547–562.

Williams, G. (1997). Reflections on some dynamics of eating disorders: "No entry" defences and foreign bodies. *International Journal of Psycho-Analysis, 78*, 927–941.

Winnicott, D. W. (1971). *Playing and reality.* New York, NY: Basic Books.

Wooldridge, T. (2014). The enigma of ana: A psychoanalytic exploration of pro-anorexia internet forums. *Journal of Infant, Child, and Adolescent Psychotherapy, 13*(3), 202–216.

Wooldridge, T. (2016). *Understanding anorexia nervosa in males: An integrative approach.* New York, NY: Routledge.

Wooldridge, T. (Ed.). (2018a). *Psychoanalytic treatment of eating disorders: When words fail and bodies speak* (Relational perspectives book series). New York, NY: Routledge.

Wooldridge, T. (2018b). The entropic body: Primitive anxieties and secondary skin formation in anorexia nervosa. *Psychoanalytic Dialogues, 28*(2), 189–202.

Wooldridge, T. (2021a). The paternal function in anorexia nervosa. *Journal of the American Psychoanalytic Association, 69*(1), 7–32.

Wooldridge, T. (2021b). Abjection, traumatic themes, and alexithymia in anorexia nervosa. *Contemporary Psychoanalysis*, *57*(2), 327–353.

Wooldridge, T., & Lytle, P. P. (2012). An overview of anorexia nervosa in males. *Eating Disorders*, *20*(5), 368–378.

Zerbe, K. (2016). Psychodynamic issues in the treatment of binge eating: Working with shame, secrets, no-entry, and false body defenses. *Clinical Social Work Journal*, *44*(1), 8–17.

Chapter 1

Alexithymia and the Psychic Elaboration of Emotion

If there is one commonality between patients with eating disorders, perhaps it is that there is disharmony in the link between body and mind. This can manifest in various ways such as, for example, the "false bodies" described in a later chapter. In this chapter, we will discuss another way that it commonly appears: difficulty putting feelings into words. Some patients may struggle to describe and elaborate on their experience, for instance, of need, desire, or hunger. While they can speak to their feelings, often quite articulately in other realms, in these particular areas this capacity is conspicuously absent. In this vein, I am reminded of one patient with a binge eating disorder who was striking for his generosity and willingness to help at home and at work; over many months, he described his efforts in this direction. As I listened, I could see that he was often exhausted, even burdened, by the time and energy he devoted to others, though he never mentioned this. His sole symptom was binge eating, late at night, alone. Over time, we discovered that binge eating was the only way he had of expressing need. He had not yet developed the capacity to speak about his need in words, to generate symbols that might express this set of feelings.

Other patients' difficulties manifest more globally, as trouble putting feelings into words that extends across most or all domains. The patient "Lucy," discussed again later in this chapter, is an example of this. Entrenched in her anorexia nervosa, she spent several months almost silent in our sessions, responding only briefly to my inquiries. Her capacity to put feelings into words was compromised in a more general way, a phenomenon often referred to as *alexithymia*.

DOI: 10.4324/9781003016991-2

Regardless of whether the difficulty putting feelings into words is circumscribed or more general, these patients may as a result have difficulty postponing action in favor of reflection. The capacity to think about, to reflect upon, difficult feelings is what allows us to forego expressing them in more problematic ways, such as, for patients with eating disorders, through a binge, or a purge, or food restriction. With this idea in mind, we will discuss the idea of *mentalisation*, which is a way of thinking about different "registers" of emotional expression and how we can identify these in patients with eating disorders, as well as the concept of reverie, which speaks to the intersubjective process that occurs between parent and child as well as between clinician and patient and that is central to facilitating the capacity to identify and elaborate emotional experience.

Alexithymia

Alexithymia, a term originated by Sifneos (1973), comes from the Greek (a = lack, lexis = word, thymus = emotion) and refers to a cluster of features including difficulty identifying and describing subjective feelings, a circumscribed fantasy life, and an externally oriented thinking style (Taylor & Bagby, 2013). Even before the 1970s, Horney (1952) and Kelman (1952) described patients who reached an impasse in treatment because of limited emotional awareness, concreteness in thinking, and a dismissing attitude toward their inner lives. Such patients were prone to developing somatic symptoms, binge eating, alcohol abuse, and other compulsive behaviors in an effort to regulate affective states. Upon its introduction as a formal construct, alexithymia was of interest to psychoanalysts engaged in the treatment of classic psychosomatic diseases. Soon, however, it became incorporated into the broader field of research on emotional processing and affect pathology (Taylor & Bagby, 2013). Since that time, it has been noted in a wide range of patient populations, including post-traumatic states (Krystal, 1968), drug dependence (Krystal & Raskin, 1970), eating disorders (Bruch, 1971, 1973, 1978), and panic disorder (Nemiah, 1984). The spectrum of disorders with which it is associated is consistent with the notion that emotion that cannot be put into words and images may generate bodily symptoms secondary to unregulated activation of bodily systems (Taylor & Bagby, 2013).[1]

Hilde Bruch (1971, 1973, 1978) recognized that patients with anorexia nervosa have a diminished capacity for "interoceptive aware-ness," that is for accurately identifying and articulating their emo-tional experience. Not only do they exhibit a profound disturbance in their ability to recognize and discriminate between feelings, but they also struggle to distinguish between emotional states and bodily sen-sations. Empirical research has since established that alexithymia co-occurs with eating disorders of all subtypes (Westwood, Kerr-Gaffney, Stahl, & Tchanturia, 2017) and with eating disorder symptomatology that does not rise to the level of an eating disorder diagnosis (e.g., Ridout, Thom, & Wallis, 2010; De Berardis et al., 2007). Even in the empirical literature, it is accepted that eating-disordered patients may use maladaptive eating behaviors (e.g., bingeing, purging, restricting) to regulate their emotions (Cooper, 2005). Whereas some studies have reported no significant differences in alexithymia across eating disor-der diagnoses, others have suggested individuals with anorexia ner-vosa experience higher levels (Nowakowski, McFarlane, & Cassin, 2013). Alexithymia appears to decrease significantly post-treatment with all eating disorders (ibid).[2]

Let us return to Lucy, a patient with anorexia nervosa. For the first several months of treatment, she was mostly silent in our twice-weekly sessions. Although she participated in her family-based ther-apy that was aimed toward weight recovery, in our meetings she seemed at a loss about what might be worth speaking about with me, though I knew, from her psychiatrist's reports, that her family was in considerable turmoil. Although her silence might have been viewed as "resistance" by previous generations of clinicians, with this under-standing of alexithymia in hand I could entertain the hypothesis that her silences might instead reflect an internal emptiness stemming from a difficulty identifying her feelings. Unable to identify her feel-ings, she tended to enact them through restrictive eating: a behavior that was, in fact, powerfully expressive. Our work, which was often slow and painstaking, was to help her develop a capacity to speak about her emotional life which, in turn, would allow her to begin to think about her feelings instead of acting them out.

Empirical research suggests that alexithymia has a multifactorial etiology, with genetic and environmental factors contributing to alex-ithymia through gene-environment interactions (Taylor & Bagby,

2013). As Fonagy (2002) suggests, it is not the actual environment that regulates gene expression but the way that the child experiences, processes, and interprets that environment. Increasingly, evidence suggests correlations between alexithymia and insecure attachment (Scheidt et al., 1999; De Rick & Vanheule, 2006; Montebarocci, Codispoti, Baldaro, & Rossi, 2004; Troisi, D'Argenio, Peracchio, & Petti, 2001) and emotional trauma (Krystal, 1988). Regarding the latter, several studies have shown that alexithymia is associated with retrospectively reported experiences of emotional and/or physical neglect or childhood sexual or physical abuse (Berenbaum, 1996; Frewen et al., 2008; Paivio & McCulloch, 2004; Zlotnick, Mattia, & Zimmerman, 2001). Other empirical studies have linked alexithymia to trauma in adulthood (Frewen et al., 2008; Taylor, 2004).

Historically, it was taken for granted that all psychic life was representational, either in words or in different kinds of imagery: visual, auditory, kinesthetic, etc. Now there is now a vast literature on unrepresented states of mind: that is, mental contents not stored in representational form as words and images but that nonetheless shape our experience and behavior (e.g., Bion, 1962; Green, 1975, 1999; Matte-Blanco, 1988; Lecours & Bouchard, 1997; Botella & Botella, 2005). The concept of alexithymia emerged as psychoanalysis was beginning to turn its attention toward unrepresented states and groups together patients for whom the capacity to symbolize and represent affect is markedly impaired. Freud (1917), with great foresight, describes affects as composite experiences that include "particular motor innervations or discharges" and "certain feelings" (p. 395). Since then, *emotion* has been defined as the neurophysiological and motor-expressive component and *feelings* as the subjective, cognitive-experiential component of *affect*, a general term encompassing both. In his writings on alexithymia, Nemiah (1977) pointed to the capacity missing in alexithymic patients: *the psychic elaboration of emotion*, through which emotions are represented mentally and experienced as feelings. This has been termed the "immune system of the psyche," for it absorbs external stresses as well as internal pressures by mentally processing their effects on the body and elaborating them further (Lecours & Bouchard, 1997).

The psychic elaboration of emotion relies upon symbolic functioning: the creation and manipulation of symbols in the form of images and language. In an early paper, Segal (1957) distinguished two modes of symbolic functioning. In the first, an object is concretely equated with a symbol, resulting in a *symbolic equation*. She provides an example of a psychotic patient who reported that he could not play the violin because he would not masturbate in public. Here, the violin is equated with the patient's penis. It does not *remind* him of his penis or conjure associations to his penis; it *is* his penis. In proper symbolic functioning, a symbol serves as a *representation* of the object (i.e., a word or image that points to it) and is not experienced as the object itself (as with a symbolic equation). It only arises through the loss of the object – a recognition of separateness from it and the mourning that entails – which leads to the recreation of the object within oneself as a symbol. In a later paper, Segal (1998) describes how a symbol becomes a *container* for the thoughts and feelings attached to the object, giving meaning to the external world.

Mentalisation

A process of *mentalisation* has been proposed to describe a preconscious (that is, operating below the threshold of consciousness) linking function that connects bodily excitations with psychic representations (Lecours & Bouchard, 1997).[3] This theory is particularly useful for it allows us to understand this process in a more fine-grained way than the binary of symbol and symbolic equation proposed by Segal (1957). The theory of mentalisation discussed here (Lecours & Bouchard, 1997) allows us to describe the relative presence or absence of the ability to put feelings into words as it manifests in the treatment situation. The notion of mentalisation was originally proposed by French psychoanalysts to understand psychosomatic patients. At that time, it implied a binary view – either experience is mentalised or not – and neglected the fact that psychic contents exist on a continuum of increasing mental quality (Lecours & Bouchard, ibid.).

Lecours and Bouchard (1997) expanded this theory to account for the never-ending transformation of psychic contents in increasing levels of complexity. Their theory draws upon two processes: representation and symbolization. The first is a process of elaborating and using a stable mental image of a thing in place of the thing itself (Sandler & Rosenblatt, 1962). The latter is a superordinate function that links already-formed mental representations as its basic building blocks (Perron, 1989). Together, these functions drive our capacity for the elaboration of bodily states into increasingly organized mental structures. In this model, this elaboration is described along two dimensions: a "vertical" dimension of four registers of expression and a "horizontal" dimension of increasing capacity for tolerance, containment, and abstraction.

The four "vertical" registers of emotional expression are somatic, motoric, imaginal, and verbal. In the somatic register, affect is expressed viscerally through internal physiological sensations, functional disturbances, and somatic lesions. In an infant, affect is first experienced as bodily excitation (e.g., pain, tension, or nausea) in the internal organs, head, musculature, and skin. Throughout development, the body remains our ultimate emotional backdrop, the place in which experience we cannot know with our minds continues to make its mark. Motor activity involves the behavior and action of the muscular body, including positive and negative manifestations (i.e., twitches and pacing and but also silences, stillness). The infant squirms, wiggles, cries, and smiles – all are reflexive enactments of a felt somatic state. Yet adults equally make use of activity as a proxy for understanding and verbalizing affect. Quatman (2015) describes a binge-eating patient who found herself eating fast food as a response to feeling taken advantage of by her husband; only when the patient was helped to translate that action into words could it be fully understood.

The imaginal, a pivotal step in the chain that bridges body and mind, involves mental imagery: mental pictures and scenes as representations of underlying bodily states. Its content takes the form of images as expressed in dreams, fantasies, and metaphors. It is a pivotal step, for it is the first register that moves from the experience of a thing in itself to a representation of that thing, which can then be elaborated further through symbolization. The verbal, finally, entails the manifestation of affect in language, in words and stories, explanations, and insights. It is the pinnacle of our emotional architecture, allowing us to link past and present, to hold up an experience and to examine it from different angles, to put our emotions "on pause," and to bridge, even if only partially, the gaps that separate us as individuals (Quatman, 2015).

The "horizontal" dimension is composed of five levels of affect tolerance, containment, and abstraction. Those levels are disruptive impulsion, modulated impulsion, externalization, appropriation of affective experience, and abstract-reflexive meaning association. At the first level, *disruptive impulsion*, affects are neither tolerated nor contained but, instead, expressed directly without mediation. In general, the subject does not "own" the affect and it will have a strong impact upon the listener. At the second, *modulated impulsion*, the discharge process is modulated, yet the affect is still impulsively evacuated from the subject's mind. The third, *externalization*, entails that an affect has begun to be tolerated and contained, undergoing some reflective activity, but not enough for it to be fully appropriated as an aspect of the subject's psychic activity. The fourth, *appropriation*, demonstrates that the subject fully tolerates the affect, experiencing it as subjective, private, and available to self-observation. The final, *abstract-reflexive*, obtains when the subject is able to make sense of what is being encountered and to subject it to complex meaning associations.

At each increasing level, the subject is protected by a "thicker" mental buffer of layers of representation and symbolization. This buffer not only dampens internal and external impacts, but it also allows for an increased capacity to subject affects to reflection and elaboration instead of immediate expression. The binge-eating patient who eats fast food without intentionally choosing to do so is operating at the level of disruptive or modulated impulsion, for her behavior is an impulsive expression of her underlying affect without reflection upon it. As she is able to put her behavior into words and, over time, to forego the behavior in favor of owning and symbolizing the underlying affect (e.g., anger at her husband), she moves toward appropriation, experiencing the anger as her own. When she is able to reflect and elaborate upon her relational pattern of feeling taken advantage of and subsequent anger expressed through masochistic behaviors, she has reached the abstract-reflexive level, the height of symbolic functioning.

In this model, alexithymia can be understood as a deficit in the capacity for mentalisation, with affects largely being expressed through the first two registers – somatic and motoric – and with little capacity for tolerance, containment, and abstraction.

Reverie

How does a child develop the capacity to mentalise? Mentalisation is fundamentally a process of *transformation* through which bodily excitations, whether somatic or motoric, undergo a qualitative transformation into mental contents within the context of human relationships (Dunn, 1995). Winnicott (1949) suggests that for infants, affect is foremost a bodily experience and that only within a "good enough" intersubjective environment – a child's relationship with his caretaker and a patient's relationship with his analyst – does the "psyche-soma," the psychic elaboration of emotional experience, begin to unfold. In this section, we now turn to Bion's (1962) ideas to better understand how the capacity to mentalise is fostered by caretakers and, by extension, how it may be promoted by clinicians working with patients with eating disorders in the consulting room.

Bion (1962) provides us with the tools to understand the intersubjective development of the capacity for the psychic elaboration of emotion or, when that development falters, of alexithymia. In his model of the mind, the development of thought is related to psychosomatic phenomena insofar as thought grows out of a matrix of bodily processes and is always derived from it. These bodily processes are a 'thing in itself' – they can never be known directly – but, through thought, they can be approached so that they can be contained by the mind for communication and thinking (Graham, 1988). Bion refers to the "thing in itself" as a *beta element*, the most primitive element of thought that lacks meaning and cannot be distinguished from bodily sensations. With beta elements, there are only two possibilities: they can be evacuated – expressed through an earlier stage on the "horizontal" dimension of mentalisation discussed earlier such that they are not appropriated as one's own and able to be reflected upon – or transformed into *alpha elements*. Alpha elements, for Bion, are the basic building blocks of thought. In the language of mentalisation, we might think of alpha elements as symbols that can be further linked and elaborated through the process of symbolization into more complex forms of mental abstraction.

How does the patient, in Bion's view, develop the capacity to generate alpha elements? It depends upon her relationship with another person. For the child, this is typically the mother, though of course other caretakers, including the father, can provide this function as well. The mother, through her *reverie* – her engagement with her own imaginative capacities – works to "decode" the child's affective expressions, whether they are somatic, such as a warmth in the cheeks or motoric, such as cries or gestures and other nonverbal cues. With her words and her responsiveness, she, over time, scaffolds the child into the world of representation. When the child cries, she says, "Oh, sweetheart, your diaper is wet," thus conveying that the child's cry has meaning. As clinicians, we seek to provide the same to our patients. We use our own mental capacities to understand and to elaborate on their distress and hope that in the process, they will internalize this capacity and increasingly be able to do this with their own creative engagement.

Again to Lucy. In one particular session, she began by telling me about a conflict that she'd had with her father the night before. After the fight, she had skipped dinner, depositing her meal into the trash while her mother was briefly away from the table. In our session, we returned to the event in detail. I asked her to recount each moment in as much specificity as she could, inquiring about the particulars of her behaviors, sensations, and thoughts. As I listened, I found myself imagining Lucy screaming in rage at her father; her anger, it seemed to me, was immense and demanded her attention. "Perhaps," I suggested, "in throwing away your meal, you were expressing how angry you were at your father." After an initial moment of protest, the idea began to resonate with her and we explored it together at length. In this brief example, I made use of my own reverie to help Lucy elaborate her feeling, previously expressed in the motoric register, into the verbal register, as a feeling of anger that she could expand in the conversation between us.

With a sketch of Bion's model in place, the development of alexithymia can be illuminated further. Krystal (1988) suggests that alexithymia results from a rupture in an individual's symbolic processes because of traumatic events in which the caretaker was not able to receive and elaborate on her infant's emotional experience. In other words, the caretaker was not, for whatever reason, able to make use of her own reverie to promote the child's capacity to make sense of emotional experience. Repeated over time, the child's developing capacity to do this for himself was undermined and, as a result, he comes to rely more upon the somatic and motoric registers for emotional expression and less upon the imaginal and verbal. In Bion's terms, alexithymia reflects a relative absence of alpha function; there is a spectrum from rudimentary toward greater complexity, the latter allowing for the possibility of more creative and innovative thought. An individual's capacity for alpha function may be radically uneven: available in some domains and absent in others. Notably, Bion suggested that beta elements are indistinguishable from bodily states, which is consistent with the alexithymic patient's difficulty making this distinction.

Notes

1   As Taylor and Bagby (2013) point out, alexithymia is a dimensional construct instead of an all-or-none phenomenon. Krystal (1982) understands alexithymia as a personality trait that has potential state variation. More recently, empirical research has provided strong support for conceptualizing alexithymia as a dimensional construct (Parker et al., 2008; Matilla et al., 2010). The implication here is that it is most useful to think of alexithymia as a continuum instead of as an all-or-nothing phenomenon. Patients may be more or less alexithymic and, equally important, may have more capacity to put their feelings into words in certain emotional states and less in others.
2   It has often been observed that because of the cognitive impairment it creates, starvation can exacerbate, or even create, an alexithymic presentation in patients with anorexia nervosa. In some cases, the capacity to describe internal states is dramatically improved by nutritional and medical rehabilitation.
3   The concept of mentalisation was introduced by French psychoanalysts in the early 1960s (Fain & Marty, 1964). Over 30 years later, the term was adopted by Fonagy and Target (1997), who conceptualized *mentalization* as the capacity to be aware of and to think about feelings and other mental states in oneself and others. This conceptualization is distinct from, though certainly overlapping with, the one proposed by Lecours and Bouchard (1997), discussed here.

References

Berenbaum, H. (1996). Childhood abuse, alexithymia and personality disorder. *Journal of Psychosomatic Research*, *41*(6), 585–595. https://doi.org/10.1016/S0022-3999(96)00225-5

Bion, W. (1962). A theory of thinking. In *Second thoughts* (pp. 110–119). London: Karnac Books (1984).

Botella, C., & Botella, S. (2005). *The work of psychic figurability*. New York: Brunner/Routledge.

Bruch, H. (1971). Anorexia nervosa in the male. *Psychosomatic Medicine, 35*(1), 31–47. https://doi.org/10.1097/00006842-197101000-00002

Bruch, H. (1973). *Eating disorders: Obesity, anorexia nervosa, and the person within*. New York: Basic Books.

Bruch, H. (1978). *The golden cage*. Cambridge, MA: Harvard University Press.

Cooper, M. J. (2005). Cognitive theory in anorexia nervosa and bulimia nervosa: Progress, development and future directions. *Clinical Psychology Review, 25*, 511–531. https://doi.org/10.1016/j.cpr.2005.01.003

De Berardis, D., Carano, A., Gambi, F., Campanella, D., Giannetti, P., Ceci, A., . . . & Ferro, F. M. (2007). Alexithymia and its relationships with body checking and body image in a non-clinical female sample. *Eating Behaviors, 8*(3), 296–304.

De Rick, A., & Vanheule, S. (2006). The relationship between perceived parenting, adult attachment style and alexithymia in alcoholic inpatients. *Addictive Behaviors, 31*(7), 1265–1270. https://doi.org/10.1016/j.addbeh

Dunn, J. (1995). Intersubjectivity in psychoanalysis: A critical review. *International Journal of Psycho-Analysis, 76*, 723–738.

Fain, M., & Marty, P. (1964). Perspective psychosomatique sur la fonction des fantasmes. *Revue français de Psychanalyse, 28*, 609–622.

Fonagy, P. (2002). The internal working model of the interpersonal interpretive function. *Journal of Infant, Child, and Adolescent Psychotherapy, 2*(4), 27–38.

Fonagy, P., & Target, M. (1997). Attachment and reflective function: Their role in self-organization. *Developmental Psychopathology, 9*, 679–700.

Freud, S. (1917). Introductory lectures on psycho-analysis. The standard edition of the complete psychological works of sigmund Freud, volume XVI (1916–1917). *Introductory Lectures on Psycho-Analysis (Part III)*, 241–463.

Frewen, P. A., Lanius, R. A., Dozois, D. J. A., Neufeld, R. W. J., Pain, C., Hopper, J. W., . . . & Stevens, T. K. (2008). Clinical and neural correlates of alexithymia in posttraumatic stress disorder. *Journal of Abnormal Psychology, 117*(1), 171–181. https://doi.org/10.1037/0021-843X

Graham, R. (1988). The concept of alexithymia in light of the work of Bion. *British Journal of Psychotherapy, 4*(4), 364–379.

Green, A. (1975). The analyst, symbolization, and the absence in the analytic setting. *The International Journal of Psycho-Analysis, 56*(1), 1–22.

Green, A. (1999). On discriminating and not discriminating between affect and representation. *International Journal of Psycho-Analysis, 80*(2), 277–316.

Horney, K. (1952). The paucity of inner experiences. *American Journal of Psychoanalysis, 12*, 3–9.

Kelman, N. (1952). Clinical aspects of externalized living. *American Journal of Psychoanalysis, 12*, 15–23.

Krystal, H. (1968). *Massive psychic trauma.* New York, NY: International Universities Press.

Krystal, H. (1982). Alexithymia and the effectiveness of psychoanalytic treatment. *International Journal of Psychoanalytic Psychotherapy, 9*, 353–378.

Krystal, H. (1988). *Integration and self healing: Affect, trauma, alexithymia.* New York: Routledge.

Krystal, H., & Raskin, H. (1970). *Drug dependence.* Detroit: Wayne State University Press.

Lecours, S., & Bouchard, M.-A. (1997). Dimensions of mentalisation: Outlining levels of psychic transformation. *International Journal of Psycho-Analysis, 78*, 855–875.

Matte-Blanco, I. (1988). *Thinking, feeling, and being: Clinical reflections on the fundamental antimony of human beings and the world.* New York: Routledge.

Mattila, A. K., Keefer, K. V., Taylor, G. J., Joukamaa, M., Jula, A., Parker, J. D., & Bagby, R. M. (2010). Taxometric analysis of alexithymia in a general population sample from Finland. *Personality and Individual Differences, 49*(3), 216–221.

Montebarocci, O., Codispoti, M., Baldaro, B., & Rossi, N. (2004). Adult attachment and alexithymia. *Personality and Individual Differences, 36*(3), 499–507. https://doi.org/10.1016/S0191-8869(03)00110-7

Nemiah, J. (1977). Alexithymia: Theories and models. In *Proceedings of the eleventh European conference on psychosomatic research.* Basel: Karger.

Nemiah, J. C. (1984). The psychodynamic view of anxiety. In R. O. Pasnau (Ed.), *Diagnosis and treatment of anxiety disorders* (pp. 117–137). Washington, DC: American Psychiatric Press.

Nowakowski, M. E., McFarlane, T., & Cassin, S. (2013). Alexithymia and eating disorders: A critical review of the literature. *Journal of Eating Disorders, 1*(1), 21.

Paivio, S. C., & McCulloch, C. R. (2004). Alexithymia as a mediator between childhood trauma and self-injurious behaviors. *Child Abuse & Neglect, 28*(3), 339–354. https://doi.org/10.1016/j.chiabu.2003.11.018

Parker, J. D., Keefer, K. V., Taylor, G. J., & Bagby, R. M. (2008). Latent structure of the alexithymia construct: a taxometric investigation. *Psychological assessment, 20*(4), 385.

Perron, R. (1989). Representations, symbolisations? *Revue Française de Psychanalyse, 53,* 1653–1659.

Quatman, T. (2015). *Essential psychodynamic psychotherapy: An acquired art.* New York, NY: Routledge.

Ridout, N., Thom, C., & Wallis, D. J. (2010). Emotion recognition and alexithymia in females with non-clinical disordered eating. *Eating Behaviors, 11,* 1–5.

Sandler, J., & Rosenblatt, R. (1962). The concept of the representational world. *The Psychoanalytic Study of the Child, 17,* 128–145.

Scheidt, C. E., Waller, E., Schnock, C., Becker-Stoll, F., Zimmerman, P., Lücking, C. H., & Wirsching, M. (1999). Alexithymia and attachment representation in idiopathic spasmodic torticollis. *Journal of Nervous and Mental Disease, 187,* 47–52. https://doi.org/10.1097/00005053-199901000-00008

Segal, H. (1957). Notes on symbol formation. *International Journal of Psycho-Analysis, 38,* 391–397.

Segal, H. (1998). "The Importance of symbol-formation in the development of the ego" – in context. *Journal of Child Psychotherapy, 24*(3), 349–357.

Sifneos, P. E. (1973). The prevalence of "alexithymic" characteristics in psychosomatic patients. *Psychotherapy & Psychosomatics, 22,* 255–262.

Taylor, G. J. (2004). Alexithymia: 25 years of theory and research. In I. Nyklek, L. Temoshok, & A. Vingerhoets (Eds.), *Emotion expression and health: Advances in theory, assessment and clinical applications* (pp. 137–153). New York: Brunner-Routledge.

Taylor, G. J., & Bagby, R. M. (2013). Psychoanalysis and empirical research: The example of alexithymia. *Journal of the American Psychoanalytic Association, 61*(1), 99–133.

Troisi, A., D'Argenio, A., Peracchio, F., & Petti, P. (2001). Insecure attachment and alexithymia in young men with mood symptoms. *The Journal of Nervous and Mental Disease, 189*(5), 311–316. https://doi.org/10.1097/00005053-200105000-00007

Westwood, H., Kerr-Gaffney, J., Stahl, D., & Tchanturia, K. (2017). Alexithymia in eating disorders: Systematic review and meta-analyses of studies using the Toronto Alexithymia Scale. *Journal of Psychosomatic Research, 99,* 66–81.

Winnicott, D. W. (1949). Mind and its relation to the psyche-soma. In *Through paediatrics to psychoanalysis: Collected papers* (pp. 243–253). New York, NY: Basic Books (1958).

Zlotnick, C., Mattia, J. I., & Zimmerman, M. (2001). The relationship between posttraumatic stress disorder, childhood trauma and alexithymia in an outpatient sample. *Journal of Traumatic Stress, 14*(1), 177–188. https://doi.org/10.1023/A:1007899918410

Chapter 2

Early Relationships, Object Relations, and Traumatic Themes

Object relations theory is concerned with how the patient's early relational experiences have been internalized as a psychological structure that continues to organize and give meaning to her experiences in the present. Are her objects "whole," reflecting both the good and bad aspects of important early relationships, or are they "parts," representations of "all good" or "all bad" experiences of intense gratification, longing, or deprivation? The objects that populate her psyche shape the anxieties with which she struggles, the longings she feels, and the defenses she erects to manage the intensities of both. From this point of view, it is the underlying psychological structure – not just the eating disorder symptoms that manifest because of it – that are a focus of treatment. The eating disorder, in other words, is a result of dynamics that are woven through the patient's personality. These ideas also provide a way for us to think about how our patients are interacting with us, moment by moment, in our work. What relational experiences are shaping her experience of us? How is this, in turn, shaping our experience of her? They inform, in addition, how we talk with our patients about both their current relationships and their histories, which is an important way that we promote their capacity to mentalise, as discussed in the previous chapter.

Gaining wide recognition, Hilde Bruch's (1962, 1973, 1978) foundational work was the first to describe anorexia nervosa in the language of object relations. For her, self-starvation represents a struggle for autonomy, mastery, and self-esteem. Disturbances in the early mother–child relationship predispose the child to develop the disorder during adolescence, a time that demands an increased capacity

DOI: 10.4324/9781003016991-3

for autonomous functioning. In her clinical work, she observed over-involved caretakers who were domineering, intrusive, and discouraging of separation and individuation. This, she argues, creates an internal confusion in children, expressed through body image disturbance (patients with anorexia nervosa tend to overestimate their body size), interoceptive disturbance (an inability to identify and respond to internal sensations, including hunger, fullness, and affective states), and all-pervasive feelings of ineffectiveness and loss of control.

Masterson (1978) suggests that patients with anorexia nervosa have a maternal object that becomes hostile and rejecting as they move toward separation and individuation and another that becomes supportive and rewarding in response to dependent, clinging behavior. Each internal representation of the mother has its corresponding self-representation – the first as bad, empty, and guilty and the second as passive, compliant, and good. Working together, these internal objects undermine patients' journeys toward adulthood, which is incompatible with the symptoms and behaviors of the disorder. Like Bruch, Masterson highlights the difficulties that patients with anorexia nervosa are having with separation and individuation. Consider, for example, "Octavia," a 17-year-old adolescent who speaks insightfully, after nearly a year of intensive clinical work, of her fear, even terror, about getting older and developing an adult body with thighs, breasts, and hips. When she imagines dating, she feels an inexplicable anxiety that, over several weeks of patient inquiry, she links to a fear that her mother will withdraw her support if she "grows up."

Other theorists have emphasized different aspects of anorexia nervosa. Some have highlighted the difficulty these patients have putting feelings into words, as discussed in the previous chapter (Birksted-Breen, 1989; Boris, 1984; Sprince, 1984). With this idea in mind, Lawrence (2001) expands on failures in symbolization and argues that mother – who is cast as dangerously intrusive – is concretely equated with food and, consequently, renounced. For the patient, emotionally, food *is* the mother, instead of evoking feelings that are *similar to* those evoked by the mother. His formulation highlights the ways in which these patients tend to form transferences shaped by this fear of intrusion, leading them to avoidantly approach the therapeutic relationship. In fact, clinicians working with this population often report feeling relationally deprived by their patients, in the same way that these patients deprive themselves. It is not uncommon for clinicians to feel that they are "pulling teeth" as they attempt to engage with some patients with anorexia. While this is often due, in part, to their difficulty putting feelings into words, it often also emerges that these patients fear that intimacy within the analytic setting will result in an unwanted intrusion.

With Octavia, for example, I notice after several weeks that she rarely allows for silence between us, filling each moment with her words. Sometimes she speaks about matters that feel emotionally important whereas, at others, it seems to me that her words lack emotional depth. It is not until I hear her speaking about the pain she feels when her mother "speaks over" her in their conversations, as if erasing her thoughts and feelings and replacing them with her own, that I begin to wonder whether the urgency in Octavia's speech with me might represent both a wish to be heard and a fear that if there were space for me to speak I might, like her mother, engage with her in an intrusive way. This theme, elaborated over many months of clinical work, is eventually also linked to her developing sexuality. "What could be more intrusive than sex?" she rhetorically asks.

There have been fewer investigations of bulimia nervosa. Masterson (1995) describes bulimia nervosa as a "closet narcissistic personality disorder." In his view, pathological grandiosity meets traumatic disappointment and the resulting psychic pain is hidden behind a defensive idealization of the other and an accompanying neglect of the self. Sugarman and Kurash (1982) propose that these patients lack object constancy: when separated from the symbiotic mother, they are unable to evoke a mental representation of her for the purposes of self-soothing. Bingeing is used to evoke a sensorimotor-based experience of the mother, akin to the patient's early experiences of childhood feeding. This formulation is consistent with the experience that many patients with bulimia describe of deriving a feeling of relief from overwhelming emotion during a binge. Sugarman (1991), in contrast, highlights the failure of these patients to communicate in symbolic form; the body, instead, is the vehicle for the expression of unconscious conflict. Other eating disorders, such as binge eating disorder and muscle dysmorphia, have received far less attention in the object relations literature, having only more recently gained wider recognition.

In the remainder of this chapter, we will discuss two traumatic themes (Shabad, 1993), or chronic patterns of frustrating and depriving childhood experience at the hands of caretakers, which take on the emotional significance of cumulative trauma (Khan, 1963). These themes were chosen because they are commonly described by patients with eating disorders. Although each will only apply to some patients – remember, eating disorders are descriptive diagnoses – these examples will clarify how underlying psychological structure, shaped by internal representations of early relationships, may manifest, symptomatically, as an eating disorder: how the eating disordered symptoms are only the tip of the iceberg, with the iceberg referring to the dynamic structure of the patient's personality as a whole. In addition, in many cases, these themes hobble the mind's ability to symbolize and represent the feelings they evoke. They may, in other words, compromise the capacity to mentalise, or put feelings into words, discussed in the last chapter.

Traumatic Theme #1: Object Hunger

One of the most common themes observed in patients with eating disorders centers on early traumatic disappointment in the child's object(s) that derails the development of an internalized representation of those objects – a key component of healthy psychological structure. In other words, because the child experience's recurrent, disappointed need for connection with an important other, he is unable to internalize that other and, over time, to provide, at least to some degree, for himself what that other might have originally provided for him. This, in turn, fuels intense object hunger which, absent intervention, persists throughout further development. The term *object hunger* has been widely used in the literature (Blos, 1967; Kohut, 1968; Ritvo, 1971; Chessick, 1985; Boris, 1984; Yarock, 1993, for examples with eating disorders). It is a desperately felt need for contact with another person who can serve as a substitute for missing segments of one's own psychic structure. This other is loved not as separate, whole person but, rather, is fervently needed to make up for what is missing internally. This yearning often has a desperate quality that may be conscious or, in contrast, vehemently defended against.

Consider, for example, the diagnosis of anorexia nervosa. Many years of clinical reports, in addition to a number of more recent empirical investigations, indicate a disturbed relationship with the mother, a distant and uninvolved relationship with the father, and a distorted sense of self. In one empirical study, anorexic patients were found to experience disrupted maternal relationships, to have a defensively overdeveloped, yet highly self-critical, sense of self, and to struggle with intense but well-defended feelings of neediness. Behind the repudiation and rejection of food and nurturance, of which these patients feel deeply undeserving, lies a powerful longing for the care and attention of the mother – in other words, object hunger (Bers, Harpaz-Rotem, Besser, & Blatt, 2013). A central task is to address not only the dangerous, self-destructive symptom of self-starvation but also the dependency needs defended against by a refusal to accept nurturance.

Freud (1938) writes, "A child's first erotic object is the mother's breast that nourishes it; love has its origin in attachment to the satisfied need for nourishment" (p. 118). Alexander (1950) affirms this notion: the child "experiences the first relief from physical discomfort during nursing; thus the satisfaction of hunger becomes deeply associated with the feeling of well-being and security." Eating is an expression of the patient's longing for comfort, which he cannot otherwise provide to himself. Yet patients with eating disorders are deeply defended against a direct recognition of their object hunger, repeating their defensive engagement with this traumatic theme in their relationship to food. Boris (1984) suggests that the hunger for food is

> a ruse, the flames of which are fanned to obscure object hunger, so food itself is a counterfeit substance to substitute for a longing for fusion – for being touched by hand and eye and voice, for being held in body and mind. (p. 319)

"Jim," for example, spends his days in a work environment that is fraught with conflict and tension. He has no conscious sense of being affected by his work environment, but over time we notice that his binge eating episodes almost always happen on the drive home after work. Perhaps, we begin to wonder, his decision to stop at a fast-food restaurant reflects his longing for comfort, for soothing from another, and, perhaps, an escape from his own anger.

Writing about patients with bulimia, Yarock (1993) suggests that these patients deny their dependency through food restriction but that this denial breaks down in a "rush of object hunger" (p. 9), leading to a ravenous appetite and a subsequent binge. Within moments, however, disgust and guilt lead to an undoing of that object hunger, manifesting as subsequent vomiting. We can also understand patients with muscle dysmorphia as seeking to turn their bodies into hard, impenetrable surfaces in a defense against a longed-for soft embrace with the maternal object. In these brief formulations, traumatic disappointment in early caretakers leads to compromised psychic structure, with object hunger signaling an urgent need to compensate for this deficit. From a young age, patients with eating disorders may begin to repeat a defensive engagement with this object hunger, shaping their developing characters and leading to particular kinds of symptom formation.

It has often been observed that eating disorders most commonly, though not solely, manifest in adolescence. Notably, adolescence is a period in which object hunger is exacerbated. Blos (1967) conceives of adolescence as a second individuation process: a phase in which the processes of the separation-individuation crisis (Mahler, 1963) are re-worked and expanded upon. Whereas toddlers in separation-individuation gain emotional supplies from the reunion with mother, adolescents are more likely to seek supplies from peers, including through the expression of their emerging sexuality in those relationships. Adolescents are notable for seeking out experiences of heightened affect, whether of excitement and elation or pain and anguish These are manifestations of object hunger, intensified in adolescence because of the concurrent lessening of parental ties as adolescents establish a greater sense of autonomy and personal identity.

Ritvo (1971), similarly, emphasizes that adolescents, impelled by emerging genital sexuality and intense object hunger, are confronted with dependence upon external objects for the gratification of these needs, for attempts to meet these needs in fantasy will inevitably prove disappointing. There is a large body of literature examining the relationship between sexuality and eating disorders (Wiederman, 1996). Confirming clinical experience, it has been found that anorexic symptoms are associated with decreased sexual activity and bulimic symptoms with increased sexual activity (Eddy, Novotny, & Westen,

2004). The anorexic is strongly defended against her object hunger whereas the bulimic's defenses against that hunger break down, leading her to over-consume and, in an effort to undo the eruption of that need, to vomit. The relationship of each of these types to their sexuality, which can be understood as a genital manifestation of object hunger, follows the same pattern. The exacerbation of object hunger and the emergence of new modes of its expression places great demand on patients with particular emotional vulnerabilities as described earlier and thus contributes, at least in part, to the emergence of disordered eating in adolescence.

Traumatic Theme #2: Breakdowns in Containment

From a psychoanalytic perspective, disruptions in early experiences with parents, especially with the mother, may constitute an important traumatic theme for patients with eating disorders. Bion (1962) describes the vital developmental function of a caregiver who can receive a child's communications of emotion that, due to the child's relative lack of psychic development, cannot be represented by the child in images or words and thought about alone. Put differently, without the caregiver's assistance, the child cannot "make sense" of what she is feeling. When all goes well, the caregiver receives these communications, attempts to make sense of them, and communicates this understanding back to the child, perhaps in words but just as often through her way of behaving with him. The child cries, for example, and the mother uses her own mind, both consciously and unconsciously, to think about the meaning of those cries and, finally, responds in a way that makes use of that understanding. Bion referred to this process between mother and child as *containment*, naming specifically the capacity to "make sense" of emotional experience as *alpha-function*. Over time, the child becomes increasingly able to perform alpha-function for himself, rendering the caregiver's capacity a persistent part of his psychological structure. Now, the child can link and organize thoughts and feelings, giving order to his internal world.

Returning to Jim. Upon analytic inquiry, we discover that his binge eating began early in elementary school, soon after he began to grapple with a persistent and troubling feeling that he was "different." It was not until his early twenties that he could articulate his feeling more clearly as conflict about his sexual orientation. The child of a conservative minister, he knew early on that his parents could not help him with these struggles. Instead, he recalls, he often lay awake feeling tormented by this sense of difference, gripped by a feeling of shame that he can only name in retrospect. His parents, we came to feel, so invested in their religious beliefs, were unable to intuit their son's distress or to comprehend the developing shape of his sexuality. This scenario constitutes a breakdown in containment, for Jim was left without the help of his parents' more developed minds in making sense of his distressing emotional experience. Instead, he came to rely upon binge eating, always done in secret, as a way of soothing his overwhelming distress.

The process of containment can break down in several ways. Bion (1962) described one scenario in which containment breaks down: when a child attempts to communicate her emotions to a parent who is impermeable or otherwise unavailable and receives them back in unmodified form, leaving the child with an experience of "nameless dread." The process of containment may also fail when a parent needs to divest herself of her own unprocessed emotional pain and so uses her child as a receptacle for it. This latter form of breakdown is discussed in *Chapter 4: Abjection and Bodily Disgust*. When containment breaks down too often, it interferes with the child's developing ability to make sense of his feelings – to mentalise, as discussed in *Chapter 1: Alexithymia and the Psychic Elaboration of Emotion*. Patients with eating disorders who have suffered this traumatic theme may thus rely upon their symptoms – restriction, bingeing, purging – to regulate affect that they cannot name, reflect upon, or communicate to another person.

References

Alexander, F. (1950). *Psychosom. Med.* New York, NY: Norton.

Bers, S. A., Harpaz-Rotem, I., Besser, A., & Blatt, S. J. (2013). An empirical exploration of the dynamics of anorexia nervosa: Representations of self, mother, and father. *Psychoanalytic Psychology, 30*(2), 188–209.

Bion, W. (1962). A theory of thinking. In *Second thoughts* (pp. 110–119). London: Karnac Books (1984).

Birksted-Breen, D. (1989). Workings with an anorexic patient. *International Journal of Psycho-Analysis, 70*, 29–49.

Blos, P. (1967). The second individuation process of adolescence. *The Psychoanalytic Study of the Child, 22*, 162–186.

Boris, H. N. (1984). The problem of anorexia nervosa. *International Journal of Psycho-Analysis, 65*, 315–322.

Bruch, H. (1962). Perceptual and conceptual disturbances in anorexia nervosa. *Psychosomatic Medicine, 24*, 187–194.

Bruch, H. (1973). *Eating disorders ed.* New York, NY: Basic Books.

Bruch, H. (1978). *The golden cage: The enigma of anorexia nervosa ed.* Cambridge, MA: Harvard University Press.

Chessick, R. D. (1985). *Psychology of the self and the treatment of narcissism.* Northvale, NJ: Jason Aronson.

Eddy, K. T., Novotny, C. M., & Westen, D. (2004). Sexuality, personality, and eating disorders. *Eating Disorders, 12*(3), 191–208.

Freud, S. (1938). *An outline of psycho-analysis.* The standard edition of the complete psychological works of Sigmund Freud, Volume XXIII (1937–1939): Moses and Monotheism, An Outline of Psycho-Analysis and Other Works, 139–208.

Khan, M. M. R. (1963). The concept of cumulative trauma. *Psychoanalytic Study of the Child, 18*, 286–306.

Kohut, H. (1968). The psychoanalytic treatment of narcissistic personality disorders: Outline of a systematic approach. *The Psychoanalytic Study of the Child, 23*, 86–113.

Lawrence, M. (2001). Body, mother, mind: Anorexia, femininity and the intrusive object. *International Journal of Psychoanalysis, 83*, 837–850.

Mahler, M. S. (1963). Thoughts about development and individuation. *The Psychoanalytic Study of the Child, 8*, 307–324.

Masterson, J. F. (1978). The borderline adolescent: An object relations view. In S. C. Feinstein & P. L. Giovacchini (Eds.), *Adolescent psychiatry* (Vol. 6, pp. 344–359). Chicago, IL: University of Chicago Press.

Masterson, J. F. (1995). Paradise lost – bulimia, a closet narcissistic personality disorder: A developmental self and object relations approach. In R. C. Marohn & S. C. Feinstein (Eds.), *Adolescent psychiatry* (Vol. 20, pp. 253–266). Hillsdale, NJ: Analytic Press.

Ritvo, S. (1971). Late adolescence: Developmental and clinical considerations. *The Psychoanalytic Study of the Child, 26*, 241–263.

Shabad, P. (1993). Repetition and incomplete mourning: The intergenerational transmission of traumatic themes. *Psychoanalytic Psychology, 10*(1), 61–75.

Sprince, M. P. (1984). Early psychic disturbances in anorexic and bulimic patients as reflected in the psychoanalytic process. *Journal of Child Psychotherapy*, *10*(2), 199–215.

Sugarman, A. (1991). Bulimia: A displacement from psychological self to body self. In C. Johnson (Ed.), *Psychodynamic treatment of anorexia nervosa and bulimia* (pp. 3–34). New York: Guilford Publications.

Sugarman, A., & Kurash, C. (1982). The body as a transitional object in bulimia. *International Journal of Eating Disorders*, *1*(4), 57–67.

Wiederman, M. W. (1996). Women, sex, and food: A review of research on eating disorders and sexuality. *The Journal of Sex Research*, *33*, 301–311.

Yarock, S. R. (1993). Understanding chronic Bulimia: A four psychologies approach. *The American Journal of Psychoanalysis*, *53*(1), 3–17.

Chapter 3

Traumatic Themes, Repetition, and Mourning

One of our central tasks with patients with eating disorders is facilitating the capacity to postpone action in favor of reflection. We inevitably find, especially early on, that this is challenging: the pull to binge, or purge, or restrict is difficult, often impossible, to resist. To understand this fact, in this chapter we begin with a discussion of Freud's (1914) notion of the compulsion to repeat and then formulate the eating disordered patient's symptoms as repetitions against traumatic themes from childhood, never-ending (because never fully successful) attempts to magically undo the pain of the past (Shabad, 1993). Ultimately, this pull toward repetition undermines the patient's capacity to direct herself – her agency. We discuss Novick and Novick's (2001a, 2016) dual-track, two-systems model of development, which provides a way of thinking about the development of agency, or its curtailment, throughout life. In this model, the open system of self-regulation is based on mutually respectful, pleasurable relationships formed through realistic perceptions of self and others. It allows for the possibility of generative creativity in love and work. The closed system of self-regulation, on the other hand, is characterized by omnipotence and a sadomasochistic stance that transforms experiences of overwhelm into hostile defense. The task with eating disordered patients is both fostering the former and ameliorating the latter.

We conclude with a discussion of mourning, which is seen as a counterpart to Freud's (1914) notion of working through. Mourning is the mechanism through which traumatic themes can be acknowledged, disillusioned wishes for an ideal object relinquished, and painful early

DOI: 10.4324/9781003016991-4

relationships transformed into aspects of the patient's character that are carried forward in constructive ways. It is an essential aspect of the treatment of patients with eating disorders that remains almost entirely unmentioned in the mainstream literature. It leads, ultimately, to the amelioration of the repetitions that have driven the patient's eating-disordered symptoms and diminished her agency.

Repetition and Traumatic Themes

In 1914, Freud published "Remembering, repeating, and working through," from which we get the often-referenced notion that what cannot be remembered will be repeated in action. Ultimately, this paper is a deep meditation on the nature of transference, that is, how the past shapes our experience in the present. Lear (2003) suggests it is Freud's most significant contribution, for if all his works were lost except for this one, it would still be possible to reconstruct what is most valuable in psychoanalysis (p. 137). A central focus with eating disordered patients is to promote the capacity to postpone action in favor of reflection. We discover, especially early in treatment, that this is challenging: the pull to binge, or purge, or restrict is difficult, and at times impossible, to resist. This pull can be understood as a *repetition of a defense against a traumatic theme from childhood, a never-ending (because never fully successful) attempt to magically undo the pain of one's past* (Shabad, 1993). The idea of traumatic themes, along with examples commonly encountered in patients with eating disorders, is discussed in both *Chapter 2: Early Relationships, Object Relations, and Traumatic Themes* and in *Chapter 4: Abjection and Bodily Disgust*. In this chapter, we will consider specifically how traumatic themes drive the process of repetition.

A child's inherent wish for a fruitful exchange with her parents can be frustrated in innumerable ways. To capture this, I use the term *traumatic themes*, which are chronic patterns of frustrating and depriving childhood experience at the hands of caretakers day after day, often for many years, that take on the emotional significance of cumulative trauma (Khan, 1963). A mother's persistent intrusiveness, or her overwhelming desire to be taken care of by her child, or her withdrawal in the face of her child's upset feelings, or a father's ongoing emotional unavailability in the face of his son's longing for connection are a few examples of traumatic themes that emerge with varying degrees of severity in the histories of these patients. The parent is likely repeating a traumatic theme from her own history that has not been mourned and, because so often repeated, has become an aspect of her character. The child is rendered helpless in his attempts to change the parent into the wished-for figure and the traumatic theme becomes an "evolving blueprint of helplessness and disenchantment before the powers of fate" (Shabad, 1993, p. 66). Faced with such experiences at a young age and without adequate emotional support through which they can be digested, the child is unable to mourn the loss of the wished-for experience with his parent, relying instead on defenses against disillusionment in this all-important relationship. These defenses, in turn, become the repetitions that, over time, etch themselves into his character.

"Mark" is a 31-year-old man who struggles with binge eating. Diagnosed with several learning disabilities at a young age, his early experiences at school left him profoundly frustrated and desperately in need of help from his parents to contend with that frustration. Yet his parents, overwhelmed with their own difficulties, often struggled to acknowledge their son's experience of need, instead communicating, at times subtly and at others more overtly, that he should be grateful for the privileges that he enjoyed. Over time, analytic inquiry suggested that Mark increasingly gave up on finding assistance in his parents and, instead, resolved to handle his difficulties on his own. By early grammar school, his neediness had been so defended against that he barely experienced it at all. His teachers, and his parents, complimented him for handling his learning difficulties with such stoicism and self-reliance. It was around this time that he began to binge eat, always at night and in secret, in the family kitchen, after his parents were asleep.

The notion of agency may be the most encompassing perspective we have of eating disorders, addressing many aspects of the struggles that we encounter clinically (Zerbe, personal communication). Agency refers to an individual's observable capacity to direct himself – or not – in a particular context: his or her local competence as an agent. This can be assessed using the clinical markers provided by Caston (2011): reversibility, self-observation, and appropriateness.[1] The compulsion to repeat is an impairment in agency, typically attenuating or negating each of these three clinical markers. Patients with eating disorders typically report little power to stop their eating disordered behaviors (i.e., reversibility), are often unaware of the thoughts and feelings they have when engaging in them (i.e., self-observation), and, by definition, their behaviors are self-defeating and fail to forward their development in constructive ways (i.e., appropriateness).

Novick and Novick (2001a, 2016) propose two distinct kinds of solutions to conflicts throughout development, captured in a dual-track, two-systems model, which offers another language for the development of agency and its derailments. Because of its emphasis on sadomasochistic patterns of relationship, this model facilities a more precise description of the dynamics frequently observed in this patient population. In a single-track model, pathology is understood to be rooted in, and used to describe, early development. Adult pathology is seen as a regression to what was normal in childhood or as an arrest in the developmental processes of childhood. In a dual-track model, an individual's strengths and impulses toward progressive development and orientation toward opportunities provided by her environment are acknowledged. Novick and Novick (ibid.) character-ize these two systems in terms of self-regulation, which includes the regulation of self-esteem. We all need to feel safe, that the world is predicable, that obstacles can be overcome, and conflicts resolved – in short, to maintain narcissistic equilibrium. When such conditions are met, infants can pleasurably engage with their environments. When faced with overwhelming experience, internal or external, they *must* find a way to restore their fragile self-esteem. Some infants, especially when faced with overwhelm that cannot be overcome, turn away from reality and toward an omnipotent solution. This learned response feels dependable and, over time, takes on an addictive quality, restricting her access to other solutions and pathways to further growth.

This *closed system of self-regulation* is characterized by omnip-otence and a sadomasochistic stance that transforms experiences of overwhelm into hostile defense. The organizing belief in this defense is of magical power to control the other and likely origi-nates in the efforts to force the mother to be "good enough" in the face of traumatic disappointment. Such omnipotent beliefs become the patient's source of self-regulation and once constructed and further consolidated in adolescence, are highly resistant to change.

The *open system of self-regulation*, in contrast, is based on mutually respectful, pleasurable relationships formed through realistic perceptions of self and others. It is open to internal and reality-based, external experiences, thus allowing for the possibility of generative creativity in love and work (Novick & Novick, 2001a, 2016). In such a system, an individual exhibits a greater degree of agency thus and her actions will be characterized by the clinical markers described by Caston (2011).

Kernberg (1995) points out, following Bruch (1962, 1973, 1978), that female patients with eating disorders often have a history of long-term, superficial submission to mother – "good girls" – while harboring deep resentment against mother's invasiveness and use of the child to bolster her own self-esteem. Their self-starvation represents a masochistic form of rebellion against mother and the assertion of autonomy under the guise of self-punishment. Many authors, including Kernberg (ibid), point out that the patient's hatred of her body is a derivative of her hatred for mother, an attempt to destroy her body as if it belonged to the mother. This closed system of self-regulation relies upon omnipotent control of the body and is an attempt to aggressively dominate the mother, with whom the patient's own body is experientially equated. Patients with anorexia nervosa often describe the addictive quality of self-starvation, for it offers them a feeling of control and power in a situation in which they would otherwise feel helpless.

Mark's binge eating also took on an addictive quality. Over time, he relied on binge eating to manage the distress evoked by the experience of need in a wide range of contexts. He experienced the behavior as entirely outside the scope of his agency, for he was utterly unable to interrupt the pattern that had plagued him since his childhood. Although our work together was extensive and involved the exploration and elaboration of numerous themes, an important thread involved slowly introducing the idea that he might have more control than he acknowledged in relation to his binge eating. Even if he was not able to stop himself on a given occasion, he did have the power to seek out various kinds of relational support, including with his analyst, and to work on developing a less conflict-ridden experience of his own need. An important aspect of this work involved the two of us noticing those moments – both inside and outside our sessions – that he experienced himself more agentically, as having a greater degree of authorship in his actions and in his life.

Indeed, viewed from a perspective of this dual-track, two systems model, technique entails elucidating the functioning of the closed, omnipotent system *and* addressing conflicts over using the open system, with the analyst maintaining the conviction that there is a possibility for genuine choice. While analysts will inevitably be drawn into sadomasochistic interactions, such a conviction helps to maintain hope and facilitates the noticing of moments, past and present, in the patient's life that have the qualities of an open system (Novick & Novick, 2001a). While a full discussion of technique is beyond the scope of this book, single-track theory can lead to technique that minimizes or ignores the role of the parents in the treatment of children and adolescents. In addition, work with parents is crucial to restoring a child or adolescent to a path of progressive development (Novick & Novick, 2001b). This is especially the case for children and adolescents with eating disorders, where parental resistance can easily stalemate a child's treatment.

Mourning as a Process of Transformation and Growth

In Freud's (1914) "Remembering, repeating, and working through," we are introduced to the notion of *working through* – the active labor of the patient, as opposed to an analytic technique – that involves recognizing (insight) and overcoming (change) resistances. In the process of working through, the patient becomes conversant with her resistances and defenses by approaching them, again and again, from different perspectives. Drawing on her will to recover, she marshals her strength to overcome these resistances and defenses and to engage with the work of remembering. In this way, she increasingly comes to rely upon remembering, as opposed to repetition, as a means of reproducing the past (Sedler, 1983). Freud describes working through as that "part of the work which effects the greatest changes in the patient and which distinguishes analytic treatment from any kind of treatment by suggestion" (pp. 155–156). In spite of the importance he assigns to the concept, he only mentions it, briefly, two additional times in his corpus (ibid).

During our second year of work together, Mark begins the session by describing how he walked into the kitchen the night before, well after midnight, and opened the fridge. While we had covered this ground many times before, this time his story took a different turn. "As I opened the fridge, I thought, 'Why am I doing this?'" Sitting at the kitchen table, he found himself beginning to cry. For the first time, he is able to emotionally link his nighttime eating to a felt sense of deprivation that originated in his early experience. Although this does not eliminate his difficulties with food, it opens a new space in which we can increasingly make emotional sense of his behavior. Over time, he continues to gain an increasing sense of agency with respect to his eating and to his health.

In this book, we have cast repetition as a repeated defense against a traumatic theme from childhood. Whether there was, in reality, an event or series of events in childhood that exceed average and expectable levels of emotional strain or whether one *interpreted* life events in such a way that they were experienced as traumatic is, in an important sense, irrelevant: the relevant events were experienced as extreme psychic pain, fear, and helplessness (Sedler, 1983). We all need to feel that the world is safe and predictable and that obstacles and conflicts can be overcome. Faced with an experience that his ego cannot sufficiently master, infants adopt a defensive stance characterized by omnipotence and sadomasochistic object relations. In my view, joined to the work of remembering is that of mourning, in which the helplessness and pain, including the disappointment with early objects, that the patient faced are directly confronted and grieved. Mourning is the vehicle of transformation through which traumatic themes can be acknowledged, disillusioned wishes for an ideal object relinquished, and painful early relationships transformed into aspects of the subject's character that are carried forward in constructive ways.

Ever since Freud's (1917) *Mourning and Melancholia*, psychoanalysis has been concerned with mourning. In that landmark paper, he attempted to elucidate the pathological mechanisms of melancholia, or depression, through comparison to mourning. This led him to the study of the superego and of structural conflict within the psyche. In his view, whereas in successful mourning the subject severs her emotional attachment to what has been lost and, thus, is free to reinvest its emotional energy elsewhere, in melancholia "one part of the ego sets itself over and against the other, judges it critically and, as it were, takes it as its object" (p. 247). This "critical agency" attacks the ego in an expression of the subject's grievance against the lost object, which it would have liked to express to that object had it not been lost.

As a brief aside, this "critical agency" is quite pronounced in patients with eating disorders. We can conceive of identification with the aggressor – that is, taking on the attributes of the originally traumatizing object – as a superego process that reflects an underlying traumatic theme. The subject remains fixated on offering herself to her parents in search of their elusive goodness and, as her bid is never accepted, it must be offered again in greater degree. When disillusionment becomes unbearable, she bridges the gap between herself and the lost parent narcissistically, by "becoming" the parental aggressor herself (Shabad, 1993). This patient population is notable for the intensity of their self-laceration. Frequent self-rebukes about weight and appearance are common, as are punishing routines of starvation or overeating. The former, for example, can be understood as a patient's identification with a caretaker by whom he felt emotionally starved, whereas the latter as an identification with a caretaker who was felt to be aggressively intrusive.

Returning to the issue of mourning, toward the end of his career Freud (1923) published *The Ego and the Id*, which is the culmination of his thinking about grief. Revising his earlier account of melancholia, he re-conceptualizes the ego as "a precipitate of abandoned object-chathexes" (p. 29), by which he means that it is effectively an embodied history of lost attachments (Clewell, 2004). Mourning, rather than coming to a decisive finale as was assumed in his earlier work, is never-ending: it is a process of transformation through which lost objects are preserved by taking them into the structure of one's own identity. These accretions are what make up the ego itself.

Hans Loewald (1989) builds upon this insight by casting mourning as an occasion for psychic integration and development. For him, the human psyche is a psychological achievement, its development making up a series of losses and reformations. The introjects that constitute the superego can, through the work of mourning, become constructive aspects of the subject's character. Internalization, an essential aspect of mourning, refers to a process of transformation through which "relationships and interactions between the individual

psychic apparatus and its environment are changed into inner relationships and interactions within the psychic apparatus" (p. 262). The
prototype of this is *eating*, in which food is lost to us (as food) but,
in the process, is transformed into something different inside of us,
whether nourishment, satiation, or indigestion and other pains (Lear,
2014). In this view, internalization is an essential aspect of psychic
growth, yet it is also a vehicle through which the ghosts of the past
may continue to haunt us.

John Bowlby (1980), father of attachment theory, recognized the
centrality of mourning in the recovery from traumatic disappointment in early objects. All forms of attachment trauma, in his view,
constitute a loss which, if not mourned, lead to "the persistent and
insatiable nature of the yearning for the lost attachment figure" (ibid.,
p. 26) – in other words, to object hunger, which is discussed as a
traumatic theme in *Chapter 2: Early Relationships, Object Relations,
and Traumatic Themes*. For Bowlby, mourning is cast as a process
through which an individual both confronts the reality of loss and
transforms representations of self as frightened, unprotected, and
helpless (George & West, 2012). He describes three forms of defense
that interact with mourning: deactivation, cognitive disconnection,
and segregated systems. Deactivation includes strategies that shift
attention away from attachment events, memories, or feelings and is
associated with evaluations of self and others as not deserving care. It
fosters "failed mourning" or "prolonged absence of conscious griev-
ing" (ibid.). Cognitive disconnection severs attachment distress from
its source, undermining the ability to hold in mind a unitary view of
events and emotions. It results in confused evaluations of the self and
others and makes it difficult to turn away from attachments. Maladaptive forms of this defense are linked to a chronic mourning state
characterized by disorganized behavior: longing for, anger toward,
and an endless search for attachment figures (ibid.). Segregated systems refer to painful and threatening attachment experiences that have
been blocked from consciousness. When this defense breaks down,
dysregulated experience and feeling manifest as a form of chronic,
pathological mourning (ibid.).

Attachment insecurity is an established risk factor for eating disorders, with estimated prevalence rates between 70% and 100%
(Ramacciotti et al., 2001; Zachrisson & Kulbotten, 2006). The Adult

Attachment Interview (AAI; Hesse, 2008) designates five adult attachment patterns: secure, dismissing, preoccupied, unresolved, and cannot classify. The majority of empirical studies conducted so far report a predominance of dismissing, which indicates a prominent use of the deactivating defense just described, and unresolved attachment, which suggests a breakdown of defense against emotional distress, in patients with eating disorders (Cole-Detke & Kobak, 1996; Fonagy et al., 1996; Ward et al., 2001; Ringer & Crittenden, 2007; Barone & Guiducci, 2009).

In one empirical study, the role of defensive exclusion (that is, of the defenses of deactivation and segregated systems) with respect to past attachment trauma was assessed in patients with anorexia nervosa using the Adult Attachment Projective Picture System (AAP; George & West, 2001, 2012). In the study, 37% of the sample was classified as dismissing, describing patients who tend to maintain an avoidant, detached, or distanced position in relation to attachment. Using the framework of traumatic themes discussed earlier in this chapter, we might formulate the situation with these patients as follows: having suffered substantial attachment trauma, they defend against object hunger by using deactivating defenses. In this way, they *repeat their defense against their traumatic themes from childhood*. With patients suffering from eating disorders, this repetition is displaced onto food, eating, and the body. The majority of patients in this study (51%) were classified as unresolved, suggesting their inability to use deactivation and cognitive disconnection strategies or to use their internal working models of attachment to manage attachment threat. Both the dismissing and unresolved patients showed evidence of traumatic segregated systems: responses to testing stimuli often contained severe, eerie, evil, or surreal material. Especially relevant for the current discussion, dismissing patients (58%) and unresolved patients (69%) were frequently found to be experiencing chronic pathological mourning (Bowlby, 1980).

This empirical study, which draws upon attachment theory and its extensive empirical literature, is brought into this chapter because it provides a distinct lens on the relationship between traumatic disappointment in early objects, repetition conceived of as a characterological defense against traumatic themes, and mourning as a process of transformation through which traumatic themes are accepted, disappointed wishes are relinquished, and painful early experiences are reintegrated as aspects of the self that may be constructively deployed in future endeavors.

Mourning continues to be an important aspect of Mark's treatment. As we build up a narrative of his history, he increasingly speaks to his grief about his childhood experience of struggling with intense frustration and need that could not be encompassed by his parents. He voices feelings of anger at his parents for failing to acknowledge and help him with his pain. As he increasingly recognizes that their limitations stem from their own histories, he speaks from a place of profound sadness, acknowledging his grief over the struggles that he has endured and the opportunities that have been foreclosed or delayed as a result. In one session, during our third year, he describes how the urge to binge eat has significantly attenuated. "I feel sadder than I used to," he remarks, "but for the first time, I also feel that I can inhabit myself. I can actually tolerate being me."

Note

1   For Caston (2011), *reversibility* refers to the range and character of power over actions within a given domain, s*elf-observation* refers to the degree of conscious focus available to and/or attendant to target actions, and *appropriateness* refers to the coherent fit of an intended action to the context in which it plays out (p. 915). In his view, these three markers serve as an operational framework for daily work with patients and apply across psychoanalytic paradigms without supplanting them. As we assess our patients' agency (or lack of it), these three markers serve as useful guides.

References

Barone, L., & Guiducci, V. (2009). Mental representations of attachment in eating disorders: A pilot study using the adult attachment interview. *Attachment and Human Development, 11*, 405–417.

Bowlby, J. (1980). *Attachment and loss: Loss, sadness and depression* (Vol. 3). New York, NY: Basic Books Classics.

Bruch, H. (1962). Perceptual and conceptual disturbances in anorexia nervosa. *Psychosomatic Medicine, 24*, 187–194.

Bruch, H. (1973). *Eating disorders ed.* New York, NY: Basic Books.

Bruch, H. (1978). *The golden cage: The enigma of anorexia nervosa ed.* Cambridge, MA: Harvard University Press.

Caston, J. (2011). Agency as a psychoanalytic idea. *Journal of the American Psychoanalytic Association, 59*, 907–938.

Clewell, T. (2004). Mourning beyond melancholia: Freud's psychoanalysis of loss. *Journal of the American Psychoanalytic Association, 52*(1), 43–67.

Cole-Detke, H., & Kobak, R. (1996). Attachment processes in eating disorder and depression. *Journal of Consulting and Clinical Psychology, 64*, 282–290.

Fonagy, P., Leigh, T., Steele, M., Steele, H., Kennedy, R., Mattoon, G., . . . & Gerber, A. (1996). The relation of attachment status, psychiatric classification, and response to psychotherapy. *Journal of Consulting and Clinical Psychology, 64*(1), 22–31.

Freud, S. (1914). Remembering, repeating and working-through. *Standard Edition, 12*, 145–156.

Freud, S. (1917). Mourning and melancholia. *Standard Edition, 14*, 243–258.

Freud, S. (1923). The ego and the id. *Standard Edition, 19*, 12–66.

George, C., & West, M. (2001). The development and preliminary validation of a new measure of adult attachment: the adult attachment projective. *Attachment and Human Development, 3*, 30–61.

George, C., & West, M. (2012). *The adult attachment projective picture system*. New York, NY: Guilford Press.

Hesse, E. (2008). The adult attachment interview: Historical and current perspectives. In J. Cassidy & P. R. Shaver (Eds.), *Handbook of attachment: Theory, research, and clinical applications* (2nd ed., pp. 552–598). New York, NY: Guilford Press.

Kernberg, O. F. (1995). Technical approach to eating disorders in patients with borderline personality organization. *Ann Psychoanalysis, 23*, 33–48.

Khan, M. M. R. (1963). The concept of cumulative trauma. *Psychoanalytic Study of the Child, 18*, 286–306.

Lear, J. (2003). *Freud* (The Routledge philosophers). New York, NY: Routledge.

Lear, J. (2014). Mourning and moral psychology. *Psychoanalytic Psychology, 31*(4), 470–481.

Loewald, H. (1989). *Papers on psychoanalysis*. New Haven, CT: Yale University Press.

Novick, J., & Novick, K. K. (2001a). Two systems of self-regulation. *Psychoanalysis and Social Work, 8*(3–4), 95–122.

Novick, J., & Novick, K. K. (2001b). Parent work in analysis: Children, adolescents and adults. Part one: The evaluation phase. *Journal of Infant, Child, and Adolescent Psychotherapy, 1*, 55–77.

Novick, J., & Novick, K. K. (2016). *Freedom to choose: Two systems of self regulation*. New York: IPBooks.

Ramacciotti, A., Sorbello, M., Pazzagli, A., Vismara, L., Mancone, A., & Pallanti, S. (2001). Attachment processes in eating disorders. *International Journal of Eating and Weight Disorders, 6,* 166–170.

Ringer, F., & Crittenden, P. (2007). Eating disorders and attachment: The effects of hidden family processes on eating disorders. *European Eating Disorders Review, 15,* 119–130.

Sedler, M. J. (1983). Freud's concept of working through. *The Psychoanalytic Quarterly, 52,* 73–98.

Shabad, P. (1993). Repetition and incomplete mourning: The intergenerational transmission of traumatic themes. *Psychoanalytic Psychology, 10*(1), 61–75.

Ward, A., Ramsay, R., Turnbull, S., Steele, M., Steele, H., & Treasure, J. (2001). Attachment in anorexia nervosa: A transgenerational perspective. *Psychology and Psychotherapy, 74,* 497–505.

Zachrisson, H., & Kulbotten, G. (2006). Attachment in anorexia nervosa: An exploration of associations with eating disorder psychopathology and psychiatric symptoms. *International Journal of Eating and Weight Disorders, 11,* 163–170.

Chapter 4

Abjection and Bodily Disgust

"Lisa" points to her thighs, which seem to me to be excruciatingly thin, and exclaims, "Can you see how disgusting these are? I can't stand to look at myself!" "Max," a young man of average weight who purges after almost every meal, laments that his stomach has always been a source of shame. "I've never lost my baby fat," he says sadly, "and I think it's gross. I'm worried that my girlfriend does, too." Patients with eating disorders commonly describe the loathing that they experience toward their bodies. They refer to their bodies, or parts of their bodies, as disgusting, ugly, gross, and fat. Although psychoanalytic thinking can contribute to our understanding of this phenomenon in numerous ways, in this chapter we will focus on Kristeva's (1982) notion of *abjection*. Kristeva's thinking is notoriously complex and difficult to grasp, so we will work through these ideas slowly, with examples, so that, with luck, it comes to life as a creative way of thinking about patients' struggles with these problems. We will also discuss two traumatic themes – a concept first introduced in *Chapter 2: Early Relationships, Object Relations, and Traumatic Themes* – that may contribute to the prominence of abjection in the experience of these patients.

Kristeva's Abject

In *Powers of Horror: An Essay on Abjection*, Kristeva (1982) presents a theoretical account of the psychological origins of the mechanisms of revulsion and disgust. The notion of the abject[1] is developed to draw our attention to those moments when we experience a frightening loss of the distinction between ourselves and objects, including people, in the

DOI: 10.4324/9781003016991-5

outer world. These moments erupt when we experience transgressions into the fragile boundaries that protect our sense of self from that which immediately threatens our sense of life. We may, for example, experience the abject when the skin that forms on the top of milk unexpectedly touches our lips or when we encounter blood, vomit, or a corpse. The abject exists outside the social world of linguistic communication and intersubjective relations and, because of this, an encounter with it disturbs identity, system, and order. Consider, in this vein, how meeting with a corpse may upend what we have taken for granted about our lives, reshaping our priorities and projects.

The abject consists of that which is taboo: horrific, monstrous elements that were once categorized as part of oneself but have now been rejected. Vomit, perhaps, is an apt example, for it was once inside of us and now, existing outside, is experienced as repellent. Kristeva (ibid) seems to understand abjection primarily in terms of bodily affect: moments of physical "discharge, convulsion, a crying out" (p. 1). In her writing, she is preoccupied with the ways in which we are both repulsed by and fascinated by these taboo aspects that have been cast out of the social order. To continue with the example of a corpse, it is something that we both want to look away from and are drawn to look at; it repulses and compels us at the same time.

In Kristeva's (ibid.) thinking, the abject is associated with the maternal, for we must successfully and violently render the maternal – the object that created us – abject in order to separate from her and to construct an identity. Yet abjection is not a stage that is passed through; rather, we are forever "abjecting subjects" (Tyler, 2009, p. 80), and all subsequent abjections contain the echo of this first, primary abjection: the infant's separation from the maternal body. To this point, Butler (2004) writes,

> We cannot represent ourselves as merely bounded beings, for the primary others who are past for me not only live on in the fiber of the boundary that contains me, but they also haunt the way I am, as it were, periodically undone and open to becoming unbounded.
> (ibid., p. 28)

Abjection, for Kristeva, is always a reminder of this primary repudiation of the maternal.

Beginning with Bruch (1971, 1973, 1978), the self-starvation characteristic of anorexic patients was seen as a struggle for autonomy from a mother that is domineering, intrusive, and discouraging of separation and individuation. Since that time, empirical evidence has supported this idea (Bers, Harpaz-Rotem, Besser, & Blatt, 2013) and difficulties with separation and individuation repeatedly emerge in psychoanalytic case studies of these patients (Ritvo, 1976; Sours, 1974; Hamburg, 1999; Lawrence, 2001; Wooldridge, 2018, 2021a to name only a few). Other eating disorders, including bulimia nervosa, have also been linked to difficulties with attachment and separation and individuation (Gander, Sevecke, & Buchheim, 2015). Given this, it is theoretically congruous that abjection, associated with the repudiation of the maternal, may be a prominent theme in many patients with anorexia nervosa and bulimia nervosa.

The image of the anorexic patient is, as Warin (2010) writes, an object of fascination, a "spectacle" (p. 9) that draws in the viewer with its lurid and shocking depiction of the female (or male) body. These images hold immense power not only to engender disgust in the spectator by confronting her with the abject but, further, in their ability to move vulnerable spectators to imitation. Ellman (1990) argues that such an image is both seductive and repellent because of its relationality: even though it seems to represent a radical negation of the other, it still depends upon that other to represent anything at all. Regardless, the anorexic patient conveys her experience of the abject through the canvas of her own body. Writing of her struggle with anorexia in adolescence, Probyn (2004) eloquently describes this experience.

> Like many, I spent much of my childhood feeling disgusting. However, any evidence of that time is scant. Of the series of photographs that document my childhood, there is an absence that occurs about the time that I was severely anorexic. The reason for the lack of previous documentation is simple: why or how could such a sight be documented? Even now my eyes turn in aversion from memories tinged with a mixture of shame, disgust, and guilt. At the same time, I do remember the splinters of pride that accompanied the disgust: pride at the beautifully prominent set of ribs, the pelvic bones that stood in stark relief, causing shadows to fall on a perfectly concave stomach. Looking back at

my experience, I wonder at the forces of pride and shame doing battle in a body that knows itself to be disgusting.

(p. 127)

As Probyn's (2004) description shows, many anorexic patients locate the abject, accompanied by the affect of disgust, at times in their own bodies and at others in the bodies of, as one patient put it, "the soft, greedy flesh" of the other, reflected in a brittle sense of pride about one's own emaciation. This oscillation, between the feeling that one's body is abject and the feeling that one has rendered her body "clean" through self-starvation and cast out infection, locating it in the other, characterizes their struggle. These patients are frequently alexithymic, as discussed in *Chapter 1: Alexithymia and the Psychic Elaboration of Emotion*, and, thus, this struggle is enacted primarily through emotional expression in the somatic and motoric registers with little capacity to tolerate, contain, and elaborate the emotions involved (Lecours & Bouchard, 1997). Were her capacity for elaborating emotion into images and words more developed, she would experience her mind as bounded, buffered by representation and symbolization, which would render her less psychically porous (Williams, 1997) and, hence, less susceptible to contagion by the abject, which has been located outside the self. This struggle, to the degree that it was present, would be contended with in language, not action.

Kristeva (1982) identifies three forms of abjection: in relation to food and bodily incorporation, to bodily waste, and to the signs of sexual difference. Indeed, she identifies the first form of abjection as "oral disgust," the most elementary and "archaic form of abjection" (p. 11), linking this observation to Freud's (1925) account of the defense of ejecting what we cannot abide, saying, "I should like to spit it out" (p. 369). Warin (2003) describes the remarkably unified, embodied reactions of anorexic patients to certain foods. In her fieldwork, she observed how certain patients "shuddered at the very thought of eating," drawing their bodies inward, closing their lips, and covering their noses and mouths (p. 83). In Kristeva's framework, this embodied reaction of closing and protecting is an effort to defend against abject horror. The fear of fat and calories, rather than stemming solely from a desire to lose weight, arises from a fear of contamination. Fats and calories are often described by anorexic patients as having the potential to engulf, contaminate, and merge, abject insofar as they threaten to "cross a border between two distinct entities or territories" (ibid., p. 75). Even as these patients desire to cast out the abject, they are simultaneously drawn toward it, as in the anorexic patient who spends hours poring over cookbooks that depict foods he will never deign to consume.

Warin (2003) describes the case of Bronte, a young woman covered in the Australian media who had a fear of "flying calories." In Bronte's words,

> One thing I remember is that when I first came in here [for treatment] I couldn't walk past anyone who was eating because. . . . I felt the calories had gone into me somehow. I'd roll up towels and push them under my door so the calories from outside couldn't come through and go into my body.
>
> (New Idea, 1997, p. 15)

Warin (ibid) evokes the miasma theory of disease common throughout the Middle Ages, in which the body was understood as permeable and highly susceptible to invasion and attack by disease, leading her to speak of "miasmatic calories and saturating fats." In my clinical practice, I have observed several anorexic patients whose fears of contagion take a different form: dread of infection with a sexually transmitted disease. Such fears, which often emerge later in recovery as a patient begins to engage more directly with his sexuality but may also be observed in some patients earlier in treatment, concern the possibility that the abject in the other could cross the self-other boundary, rendering the self infected and, thus, repellent.

The abject is frequently experienced in relation to sexuality in other ways. Warin (2003) points out that anorexic women frequently describe their bodies – reproductive, digestive, and sexual – in the same ways they describe food, as dirty, polluting, and dangerous. Menstruation and digestion are often recounted with great detail and disgust. One of my male patients with anorexia was terrified that his semen would be stolen and used to impregnate an unknown woman or, even worse, to substantiate allegations of rape against him, both of which, in his mind, would reveal his abjection to the world, including his entanglement with the maternal.

The history of eating disorders begins at least with ascetic medieval saints who, like the modern anorexic teenager, scrutinized every desire for its purity or lack thereof (Bell, 2014). The anthropologist Mary Douglas (2003) argues that purity, far from being based on the fear of "germs," is a means of differentiating some phenomena from other phenomena, whether bodies from bodies, castes from castes, or races from races. These laws of purity are, most often, a ritual repudiation of what reminds us of the body of our mother – menstrual blood, mucus, etc. Rituals are designed to exclude any reminders of maternal dependence, which is abject and threatens to disrupt our sense of identity and order.

In the modern era, many young anorexic women express strong associations between their own bodies and their mothers' bodies, wishing to forestall or prevent entirely further development of similarities to them: the growth of hips, thighs, breasts. More generally, food and sexuality are feared because of the connections they imply to other people (Warin, 2003). Numerous patients with eating disorders refuse to eat with their families and friends, even insisting on eating only in private. Many of the practices that are seen as essential for creating and sustaining relatedness – the sharing of food, living together, sexual relationships, and even reproduction – are consistently negated by anorexic and other eating disordered practices.

Roots of the Abject Self: Foreign Bodies

In *Chapter 2: Early Relationships, Object Relations, and Traumatic Themes*, we discussed the prominence of traumatic themes (Shabad, 1993), or chronic patterns of frustrating and depriving childhood experience at the hands of caretakers, in the histories of patients with eating disorders. In the remainder of this chapter, we will discuss two traumatic themes that are commonly observed in patients with eating disorders for whom the experience of abjection is prominent. These themes are specific aspects of a larger pattern frequently observed in the literature: the mother's use of the developing child to maintain the stability and coherence of her own sense of self and to regulate her self-esteem (Bruch, 1971, 1973, 1978; Birksted-Breen, 1989; Williams, 1997).

In this section, we return to the idea of breakdowns in containment, first discussed in *Chapter 2*. As you may recall, Bion's (1962) theory of containment describes how the mother uses her own mind to make sense of her child's emotions, for the child lacks the ability to do so on his own. Both through her words and how she behaves with him, she conveys that his emotions have meaning. In healthy development, over time this fosters the child's ability to increasingly make sense of his emotions on his own. In this way, he internalizes his mother's containing capacity.

This process can fail in various ways. Bion (1962) describes one scenario: when a child attempts to communicate his emotions to a parent who is impermeable or otherwise unavailable, leaving the child with an experience he evocatively calls "nameless dread." Williams (1997) describes another way in which containment may break down: when parents need to divest themselves of their own emotional pain, which cannot be adequately managed within their own minds, and instead use the child as a receptacle for it. In this situation, the child tends to experience the parental divestment as a type of *foreign body* inserted into her mind, which serves as a receptacle. Lawrence (2001), along these lines, argues that the mother is experienced as dangerously intrusive and is concretely equated with food. The patient cannot think about how food is experienced *like* the mother; rather, at an emotional level, it feels that food is intrusive because it *is* the mother. Lawrence's formulation highlights the ways that patients with anorexia tend to form transferences shaped by the fear of intrusion, leading them to avoidantly approach the analytic relationship. This is consistent with the experience reported by many clinicians of feeling relationally deprived by anorexic patients, in the same way that the patient deprives herself.

In her article, Williams (1997) describes a class of "psychically porous" patients who suffer from eating disorders, most frequently bulimia nervosa, and suggests that they had parents who themselves suffered extensive traumas and as a result were either frightening or frightened or both in relation to the child. Such parents are more likely to divest their anxiety than to contain it. Williams' description of her patient, Daniel, is as follows:

> Describing his bulimia, Daniel conveyed a vivid perception of being full of inimical foreign bodies. When I started seeing him he was bingeing and vomiting up to six times a day. He was

tormented by concrete bodily feelings, of being "all dirty inside". Blocked sinuses and nose contributed to his perception. He said he felt "greasy", "full of soot", "disgusting". Vomiting gave him very temporary relief.

He binged on anything he could find or buy with his limited pocket money allowance. He bought mostly loaves of white bread which, he said, was "like blotting paper". It soaked up "all the nasties" that could then be got rid of by vomiting. After being sick, he felt temporarily "clean inside". His mind became clear and for a few hours he could apply himself to his studies. Then "the buzz", as he called it, would start again. When "the buzz" started, Daniel was unable to concentrate. . . . He described "the buzz" as "thoughts racing through his mind at 150 miles per hour". It became clear that they were not thoughts he could think or talk about, but something more akin to flying debris.

(p. 930)

Daniel's felt himself to be "all dirty inside," a concrete experience of having been the receptacle for his mother's anxiety. This led him to expel, through vomiting, those toxic foreign bodies – soaked up by the "blotting paper" of white bread – which left him, temporarily, feeling "clean inside." Before long, however, the cycle starts again. In fact, Williams (1997) suggests that patients such as Daniel have internalized a parent overflowing with projections, which exerts a disorganizing impact on their internal worlds (i.e., the "buzz" that he describes).

For Williams (1997), many patients with anorexia nervosa have been subjected to the same experience of being used as a receptacle for their parents' unprocessed anxieties. Unlike psychically porous patients with bulimia nervosa, however, these anorexic patients have developed a "no-entry system of defense" that covers over their experience of having been permeable in this way. This no-entry system of defense consists of a defensive rejection of input not confined to food intake but manifesting across the patient's character. Along the same lines, Zerbe (1993) observes that the refusal of food is "an autonomous statement, par excellence: "I don't need you. I don't need anything. I don't even need food to survive. I am totally independent" (p. 95). Chasseguet-Smirgel (1993, 1995), similarly, suggests that anorexic patients attempt on the level of unconscious fantasy to function in an autarchical manner, completely without the need of nourishment, literal and figurative, from external sources, especially the early, primary object.

These ideas are also illustrated with "Sara," a patient in analytic treatment with anorexia nervosa who is also discussed in *Chapter 5: Body–Mind Dissociation and False Bodies* and *Chapter 9: Eating Disorders in Cyberspace*. Born profoundly premature, she was subjected to numerous surgeries early in life and her family lacked the capacity to contain the intense distress aroused in her by these experiences. Early in treatment, she described how every thought shared with me held the potential to be used as a sharp instrument that could pierce her psychological skin. Such statements reflected the contribution of her early trauma in shaping our experience together, insofar as she felt herself to be, once again, a young child who was intensely vulnerable before an adult who repeatedly invaded her delicate internal space. In trying to help her find relief, I risked hurting her, and in fact during substantial periods of the treatment I found that despite my efforts to craft sentences that were gentle and curious, my comments often had an unintentionally sharp edge. I came to dread the experience of feeling that my words hurt this woman whose physical appearance conveyed such profound fragility, yet for several years I could not find a way of engaging with her, over an extended period, that avoided it.

The experience of being heavily projected into in the countertransference alerts us to the possibility that the patient might have been at the receiving end of massive projections in early development (Grinberg, 1962). In addition to trauma originating in prematurity, Sara's mother frequently made use of her as a receptacle for her own unprocessed anxieties. Around age eight, for example, she was eating a pear in her family's kitchen when her mother walked in and noticed pear juice running down her daughter's chin. She became distraught and insisted that Sara explain what, in her mind, was an overt exhibition of sexuality. Her mother's need to divest herself of her own psychotic anxieties about sexuality left her feeling "filled up" with toxic shame and disgust with her physicality. This intensified at puberty when boys began to show an interest in her and her body became more curvaceous. Throughout treatment, we discussed her visceral disgust with her sexuality and those aspects of her body that she associated with it: breasts, thighs, genitals.

Although this treatment was extensive and aspects of it have been described at greater length elsewhere – in particular, there was a great deal of work put into establishing a treatment team (Novack, 2021; Wooldridge, 2021b) and facilitating medical and nutritional rehabilitation – I wish to emphasize the slow, painstaking work that was required for Sara to develop her capacity to represent and symbolize (Lecours & Bouchard, 1997) her experience, to put her feelings into words. At several points, I found that my attempts to put words to her distress recreated the experience of being "filled up" by ideas that she could not yet digest, which led to her experiencing me (accurately, to some degree) as a persecutory figure. Each time, after a difficult period of repair between us, I sought to attune myself more accurately to what she could, and could not, tolerate thinking about. At other times, I struggled to find words for her experience, for the horror of certain aspects of her childhood was simply too much to encompass. Yet after several years of work on this, her capacity for the psychic elaboration of emotion (Nemiah, 1977) significantly more developed, what she was previously only able to describe in impoverished, concrete terms – fat, disgusting, repellent – she was now able to express in complex, multi-faceted narratives about her experience. Though treatment is still ongoing at the time of writing, Sara has maintained her physical health for many years and is now productively engaged with her inner and outer life.

Roots of the Abject Self: Rotten Core

The second traumatic theme I have observed in anorexic patients for whom the experience of abjection is prominent is the formation of a *rotten core*: a feeling of inner rottenness that lies hidden behind an adaptively functioning, outer self (Lax, 1980). This theme, once again, occurs within a larger context in which the mother has marked vulnerabilities that manifest in relation to her developing child. The rotten core may develop when mother becomes severely depressed, or otherwise emotionally unavailable, during the patient's toddlerhood. In particular, the rapprochement subphase of development – already a difficult period in the life of the toddler – is cast as the time when the toddler is most vulnerable to the development of this form of self pathology. The rapprochement subphase was first described by Mahler as a developmental phase of the separation-individuation process in which the toddler develops a new awareness of her separateness from her caregiver and struggles with the simultaneous need for both autonomy and support (Mahler, 1972). In this subphase, "practicing" – the child's "love affair with the world" – has come to an end. The child now contends with a wish for reunion with the mother and a fear of being engulfed by her. Only mother's loving acceptance of her child, a good enough combination of ambivalence and encouragement, leads to a healthy resolution of this crisis.

For Lax (1980), the rotten core develops in response to the mother's emotional unavailability to her child during this period, frequently due to depression, which the child interprets as anger. Since the toddler is unable to comprehend the objective origins of the mother's emotional unavailability, he regards his own strivings as the cause of it. He may even regard this unavailability as punishment. This, in turn, interferes with the normal processes of separation and individuation, especially if he begins to regard his impulses toward autonomy with the disapproval ascribed to mother. At its most primitive level, the rotten core represents the fusion of the "bad" (angry-rejecting) maternal introject with the "bad" (rejected) aspects of the self. The rotten core represents that part of the self that was "hate-able" to the mother. This typically exists alongside an experience of self and mother as good and lovable.

Most relevant to the formation of a rotten core are situations in which mother's intensified needs for closeness lead to an invasion of the child's autonomy and the foreclosure of his attempts to explore the world and when the mother's capacity for object constancy – that is, to maintain a sense of both her good feelings and bad feelings toward her child at the same time – breaks down, leading her to experience the child as either all good or all bad (Lax, 1980). "Adam" is a patient seen for nearly eight years in an analytic treatment, beginning nearly ten years after "recovery" from anorexia nervosa but still plagued by difficulties.[2] He remembered a mother who was at times intensely engaged with him, implicitly conveying that he was the center of her universe, whereas at other times she became wounded by his need and withdrew into her room, leaving him alone for hours. Over time, we came to suspect that his expressions of need, often provocatively insistent, as a child may have been attempts to turn incomprehensible hostility into comprehensible anger.

In our early work together, Adam frequently voiced complaints about his body shape and size, reporting that he experienced his body on some days as "utterly disgusting" and on others as "fine, even good." This former experience of his bodily self is an expression of the fusion of the "bad" (angry-rejecting) maternal introject with the "bad" (rejected) aspects of the self, though these affects remained in an unsymbolized, unrepresented form (Lecours & Bouchard, 1997). The rotten core is established as a permanent psychic structure because of the child's identification with the maternal attitude toward him, which fosters an identical attitude toward the self. Aspects of the self unacceptable to the mother are rejected by the child and merge with the primitive rotten core toward which the combined mother-child hatred has been directed (Lax, ibid). This identification with the aggressor gains further strength from the wish to obtain mother's love. Adam's eating disorder was, among other things, an alexithymic expression of mother's rejection of his need, which he had identified with and enacted upon his needy, bodily self (Sands, 2003).

Adam described several relationships with women who treated him poorly, including his current wife. Though deprived of relational nourishment in numerous ways in his marriage and often quite angry about these deprivations, he nevertheless remained deeply attached, in a rather symbiotic way, to his wife and committed to their marriage. Over time, analytic investigation revealed an unconscious fantasy of an idealized mother who would gratify him in every conceivable way: the good symbiotic mother (Mahler, Pine, & Bergman, 1975). This fantasy had persisted into adulthood because the reality of his mother's poor treatment of him was explained by the conviction that it was caused by his inability to evoke her goodness because of his inner rottenness. "Bad" behavior, in both fantasy and reality, was used to explain mother's aggression. In this sense, his wife's treatment of him felt "right" and served to spur on his efforts to be a "better husband." As Lax (ibid.), points out, this masochistic relational stance is fueled by a fantasy that sufficient suffering will bring atonement and rescue by the good mother.

Adam, healthier at the beginning of treatment than the other patients discussed in this chapter, nevertheless presented with impairments in his capacity to symbolize and represent affects, especially those pertaining to the traumatic theme of the rotten core (Lax, 1980). His impairment was less broad than that of other patients with anorexia for whom the capacity for the psychic elaboration of emotion (Nemiah, 1977) is more generally compromised and who are often described as alexithymic. And in contrast to the ruptures that occurred in the treatment of Sara previously discussed, Adam and I were consistently, even enthusiastically, engaged in the work of being able to "think together," although much of what we thought about was painful and evoked a prolonged mourning process. Had we worked together during the height of his anorexia, I suspect, based on an extensive reconstruction of his history, that his impairment, too, would have been more general and that our treatment would have been more difficult, with more risk of alliance ruptures. Despite his greater health, however, the traumatic theme of the rotten core created a traumatic organization that repetitively manifested, in unrepresented and unsymbolized form, in Adam's experience of his body and in his relationships with women.

Notes

1 The term "abjection" also commonly appears both as an adjective ("abject women") and as an adjective turned into substantive ("the abject") (Menninghaus, 2003).
2 Epidemiological data suggests that as much as 25% of the anorexic population is male (Hudson, Hiripi, Pope, & Kessler, 2007).

References

Bell, R. M. (2014). *Holy anorexia*. Chicago, IL: University of Chicago Press.

Bers, S. A., Harpaz-Rotem, I. Besser, A. Blatt, S. J. (2013). An empirical exploration of the dynamics of anorexia nervosa: Representations of self, mother, and father. *Psychoanalytic Psychology*, *30*(2), 188–209.

Bion, W. (1962). A theory of thinking. In *Second thoughts* (110–119). London: Karnac Books (1984).

Birksted-Breen, D. (1989). Workings with an anorexic patient. *International Journal of Psycho-Analysis*, *70*, 29–49.

Bruch, H. (1971). Anorexia nervosa in the male. *Psychosomatic Medicine*, *35*(1), 31–47.

Bruch, H. (1973). *Eating disorders: Obesity, anorexia nervosa, and the person within*. New York, NY: Basic Books.

Bruch, H. (1978). *The golden cage*. Cambridge, MA: Harvard University Press.

Butler, J. (2004). *Precarious life: The powers of mourning and violence*. London: Verso.

Chasseguet-Smirgel, J. (1993). Troubles alimentaires et feminité: Reflections à partir de cas d'adultes ayant présenté des troubles alimentaires à adolescence [Eating disorders and femininity: Some reflections on adult cases that presented an eating disorder during adolescence]. *Canadian Journal of Psychoanalysis*, *1*, 102–122.

Chasseguet-Smirgel, J. (1995). Auto-sadism, eating disorders, and femininity: Based on case studies of adult women who experienced eating disorders as adolescents. In M. A. F. Hanly (Ed.), *Essential papers on masochism*. New York, NY: New York University Press.

Douglas, M. (2003). *Purity and danger: An analysis of concepts of pollution and taboo*. New York: Routledge.

Ellman, M. (1990). Eliot's abjection. In J. Fletcher & A. Benjamin (Eds.), *Abjection, melancholia and love*. London: Routledge.

Freud, S. (1925). Negation. *The International Journal of Psychoanalysis*, *6*, 367–371.

Gander, M., Sevecke, K., & Buchheim, A. (2015). Eating disorders in adolescence: Attachment issues from a developmental perspective. *Frontiers in Psychology*, *6*, 1136.

Grinberg, L. (1962). On a specific aspect of countertransference due to the patient's projective identification. *International Journal of Psycho-Analysis*, *43*, 436–440.

Hamburg, P. (1999). The lie: Anorexia and the paternal metaphor. *Psychoanalytic Review*, *86*, 745–769.

Hudson, J., Hiripi, E., Pope, H., & Kessler, R. (2007). The prevalence and correlates of eating disorders in the national comorbidity survey replication. *Biological Psychiatry*, *61*, 348–358.

Kristeva, J. (1982). *Approaching abjection, powers of horror* (pp. 1–31). New York, NY: Columbia University Press.

Lawrence, M. (2001). Loving them to death: The anorexic and her objects. *International Journal of Psychoanalysis*, *82*, 43–55.

Lax, R. (1980). The rotten core: A defect in the formation of the self during the rapprochement subphase. In R. Lax, S. Bach, & J. A. Burland (Eds.), *Rapprochement: The critical subphase of separation-individuation*. New York, NY: J. Aronson.

Lecours, S., & Bouchard, M.-A. (1997). Dimensions of mentalisation: Outlining levels of psychic transformation. *The International Journal of Psychoanalysis*, *78*, 855–875.

Mahler, M. S. (1972). Rapprochement subphase of the separation-individuation process. *The Psychoanalytic Quarterly, 41*(4), 487–506.

Mahler, M. S., Pine, F., & Bergman, A. (1975). *The psychological birth of the human infant*. New York: Basic Books.

Menninghaus, W. (2003). *Disgust: Theory and history of a strong sensation* (H. Pickford, trans.). Redwood City, CA: Stanford University Press.

Nemiah, J. C. (1977). Alexithymia: Theoretical considerations. *Psychotherapy and Psychosomatics, 28*(1–4), 199–206.

New Idea (1997). *Bronte's miracle cure*. November 28, pp. 14–17.

Novack, D. (2021). "It takes a village": Concurrent eating disorder treatment and the multiperson field. *Psychoanalytic Dialogues, 31*(2), 181–196.

Probyn, E. (2004). *Carnal appetites: Food sex identities*. London: Routledge.

Ritvo, S. (1976). Adolescent to woman. *Journal of the American Psychoanalytic Association, 24*, 127–137.

Sands, S. (2003). The subjugation of the body in eating disorders: A Particularly female solution. *Psychoanalytic Psychology, 20*(1), 103–116.

Shabad, P. (1993). Repetition and incomplete mourning: The intergenerational transmission of traumatic themes. *Psychoanalytic Psychology, 10*(1), 61–75.

Sours, J. A. (1974). The anorexia nervosa syndrome. *International Journal of Psychoanalysis, 55*, 567–576.

Tyler, I. (2009). Against abjection. *Feminist Theory, 10*(1), 77–98.

Warin, M. (2003). Miasmatic calories and saturating fats: fear of contamination in anorexia. *Culture, Medicine and Psychiatry, 27*(1), 77–93.

Warin, M. (2010). *Abject relations: Everyday worlds of anorexia*. Piscataway, NJ: Rutgers University Press.

Williams, G. (1997). Reflections on some dynamics of eating disorders: "No entry" defenses and foreign bodies. *International Journal of Psycho-Analysis, 78*, 927–941.

Wooldridge, T. (2018). The entropic body: Primitive anxieties and secondary skin formation in anorexia nervosa. *Psychoanalytic Dialogues, 28*(2), 189–202.

Wooldridge, T. (2021a). The paternal function in anorexia nervosa. *Journal of the American Psychoanalytic Association, 69*(1), 7–32.

Wooldridge, T. (2021b). Alexithymia, meaning-making, and management: Response to Novack. *Psychoanalytic Dialogues, 31*(2), 197–204.

Zerbe, K. J. (1993). *The body betrayed: Women, eating disorders, and treatment*. Washington, DC: American Psychiatric Press.

Chapter 5

Body–Mind Dissociation and False Bodies

For Ferrari (2004), the body–mind link begins to develop when the earliest experience of the physical body, the *onefold*, is taken as the mind's first object. Through successive mental elaboration, it manifests in its mental expression, the *twofold*, whose primary function is to contain the sensory stimuli that emanate from the body (Lombardi, 2009). This successive mental elaboration is facilitated through the mother's reverie, as described in *Chapter 1: Alexithymia and the Psychic Elaboration of Emotion*. When this reverie is interrupted or inadequate – when there is a breakdown in containment, as considered in previous chapters – one potential consequence is an impairment in the ability to put feelings into words, as we have discussed. In this chapter, we turn to another way in which the body–mind link may be disrupted: the development of a false body. The term *false body* refers to the way that the body's state is rigidly controlled such that spontaneous emotional experiences are foreclosed. Because the body's experience is kept within tight parameters, emotional experiences, fundamentally grounded in the body and potentially catastrophic if experienced outside the context of relational support, are kept out of awareness.

For some patients with binge eating disorder, the weight gain that results from eating symptoms may serve as a false body. The experience of being overweight may, for example, stifle desire, need, and longing. As one patient put it, "When I'm overweight, my sexuality shuts down. I know that I'm not desirable and I'm so filled with self-loathing that I don't feel desire." Efforts to lose weight resulted in the return of desire, which was experienced as emotionally overwhelming

DOI: 10.4324/9781003016991-6

and undermined her weight loss efforts. Goldberg (2004) describes how patients – who might be described as *orthorexic*, a term which though not in the diagnostic manuals is nonetheless increasingly used to refer to an unhealthy focus on eating in a healthy way – may use seemingly healthy exercise regimes, including a rigidly controlled diet and obsessive self-care rituals, to maintain a false body. Another patient described to me how after her two-hour morning yoga session, she remained so exhausted throughout the day that she was unable to feel anything. Her feelings, we came to learn, were disturbing for they were not under her immediate control.

In the remainder of this chapter, we discuss a particular form of the false body that is commonly observed in patients with anorexia nervosa called the entropic body (Wooldridge, 2018). The *entropic body* is cultivated through self-starvation and rigidly maintained to subjugate an underlying emotional experience of need and dependence. It develops as a "best attempt" to compensate for the failure to internalize the caretaker's capacity to comfort and soothe the child during the period of separation and individuation. Without the capacity to provide comfort to oneself or to seek it in emotional connection with another person in hand, these patients are unable to emotionally "digest" traumatic experiences in infancy and beyond. The fear of getting "fat," commonly expressed by patients with anorexia nervosa, conveys the emotional agony that results from having to contend with these undigested traumatic experiences. These ideas will be illustrated with reference to an extended case presentation of "Sara," a young woman with anorexia nervosa.

Breakdowns in Containment: A Clinical Example

In this section, we will focus on "Sara," a young woman in her late teens who has been seen for many years in twice-weekly analysis for a severe case of anorexia nervosa. In what follows, we will see the traumatic theme of breakdowns in containment, first discussed in *Chapter 2: Early Relationships, Object Relations, and Traumatic Themes*, as revealed through her recollections and reconstructions of early experiences after a traumatic birth as well as difficulties in the relationship between mother and child. In addition, we will explore how this theme was repeated, and ultimately repaired and worked through, in the relationship between patient and analyst.

Sara was born approximately six weeks premature, and according to her father, the family was uncertain for several weeks whether she would live. For a substantial period, her life was maintained in an incubator, isolated from human contact. Through latency, she suffered from numerous of physical complaints, including fatigue, stomach pain, and headaches. She remembers innumerable visits to doctors and hospitals, and several invasive procedures, including colonoscopies and endoscopies, were performed.

In the early months of treatment, Sara would become angry and withdrawn when I suggested possible meanings to her associations. These interactions culminated on several occasions with her curling up tightly in her chair, yelling that I was "cold and cruel" while tears ran down her face. This situation, in which my interpretations seemed to evoke her early wounding, led to an impasse that persisted for several months. Despite my efforts to craft sentences that were gentle and curious, my comments often had a subtly sharp edge. I came to dread the experience of feeling that my words hurt this woman whose physical appearance conveyed such profound fragility, yet I could not find a way of engaging with her, over an extended period, that avoided it.

But one Friday afternoon Sara made a comment that brought us out of a prolonged and deadened silence, and my thinking began to shift. Looking at me without expression, she said, "It's like I'm giving you weapons that you can pierce me with." Certainly, this statement reflected the contribution of her early trauma in shaping our experience together. My interpretations felt "piercing" in the same way her earliest experiences with medical doctors had been. I continued to worry about how much she suffered in our sessions. In trying to help, I seemed to be hurting her. I often imagined her early life in an incubator, in which light and sound would have been experienced as overwhelming. And I envisioned myself as a well-intentioned physician who, in trying to save her life, pierced her skin with needles. At times, this experience of myself was overwhelming.

The clinician's experience of receiving overwhelming projections in the countertransference often reflects the patient's experience of having to contend with intrusive projections in early development (Grinberg, 1962). While Sara's medical history helped to explain what was happening between us, we soon learned that her early emotional life had been marked in this way. She remembered one incident that represents the intensity of her mother's projective identifications (that is, of putting her own undigested emotional experiences into her daughter). Around age eight, she had been eating a pear in her family's kitchen. When her mother walked in and saw "the juice running down [Sara's] chin," she became distraught and insisted that her daughter explain what, in her mind, was an overt exhibition of sexuality. Her mother's need to divest herself of her own psychotic anxieties left Sara feeling "filled up" with toxic shame. This was prototypical of many of her childhood experiences in her family.

As previously considered, anorexia nervosa can be understood, in part, as stemming from a breakdown in containment in early life (Bion, 1962). In some forms of breakdown, in which the child is used as a receptacle for the mother's own unprocessed emotions, a system of defenses develops that is characteristic of anorexia nervosa. Williams (1997) describes this as the "no-entry" system of defenses: an effort to keep things from "getting inside" that stems from earlier experiences of traumatic intrusion. As we soon learned, Sara was subjected to intense physical and emotional intrusion throughout her childhood. As a result, the experience of nourishment, of "taking in" – both physical and psychical – was terrifying to her in all areas of her life. To protect her vulnerable and needful self, she was determined to not let anything get inside. She was terrified of physical manifestations of penetration and avoided sexual contact. She had never received a gynecological exam.

This relational pattern dominated the analysis for the first year. In such situations, it is imperative for the analyst to examine her own emotional history to understand what she might be contributing to such an impasse. During this time, I spent innumerable hours wondering why I continued to find myself speaking with a sharp edge, despite my best efforts to remain curious and empathic. I recognized that I was relying too heavily on my intellect, but why? My impression of Sara in our first meeting had been a deep sense that something catastrophic had happened to her. With difficulty, I had pushed that thought aside for fear that it would make it impossible for me to help her. In a situation where life and death hung in the balance, how could I maintain equanimity? I inhabited my intellect because the emotional experience of being with her catastrophic experience was overwhelming to me. With the help of ongoing self-analysis and consultation, I was able to encompass the extent of her suffering more fully, including the catastrophic pain of her early life and the ongoing repetition of that catastrophe in our relationship, here and now.

The following Monday, the treatment began to move again. Sara began the session with a cold stare. I said, "I'm wondering if last Friday's session is still on your mind. I could see how you'd still be upset with me for hurting you." After a brief look of confusion, Sara said, "Yes, that's right." I responded that it was my hope that we could find a way to be together that hurt less, and that while I knew it would take a lot of work, I hoped she would join me in that endeavor. And though there was no overt acknowledgment from her beyond a simple nod and restrained smile, I could sense that something in her had softened. She continued to struggle with taking in nourishment – both literal and metaphorical – but now we were joined in struggling together.

It was during this period that Sara began to follow her nutritional plan more regularly and regained a substantial portion of the weight. By the second year, she was no longer in immediate medical risk. And our work began to deepen as more primitive anxieties emerged during the second year of treatment, to which we will now turn.

Annihilation Anxiety

As Sara and I continued, I was struck by the fact that she filled every moment of her life with work, deploying a complex array of manic defenses to avoid the feelings lurking beneath the surface. In an early conversation, she mentioned the possibility of trying to slow down, and I remarked that I thought this would be difficult for her. In response, she began to describe a feeling of "shattering" that she worried she might encounter if she slowed down. This was an expression of *annihilation anxiety:* the fear that the integrity of the self is threatened. Traumatic themes (Shabad, 1993), chronic patterns of frustrating and depriving childhood experience at the hands of caretakers, such as those discussed in *Chapter 2: Early Relationships, Object Relations, and Traumatic Themes*, may undermine the cohesion and differentiation of the developing self. When there are extreme deficits in the cohesion and differentiation of the self-structure, certain threats may even lead to an experience of the dissolution of the self (Kohut, 1977).

In adult life, anxiety becomes associated with a dread of returning to this infantile trauma and, in fact, with the expectation that it will recur. In a brief yet potent paper, Winnicott (1974) discusses the fear of breakdown. His thesis is startlingly simple: The patient's fear of breakdown is, in fact, the fear of a breakdown that has already happened. It is a fear of the original agony – anxiety, he notes, is not a strong enough word – that caused the defensive organization of the patient's character. Until the patient can gather into the present what happened in the past so that it can be experienced completely, the catastrophe will always recede into the future.

Freud (1926) describes a sequence of "danger situations" that he imagined might feel like threats to the structure and integrity of the self (Horner, 1980). These include overwhelming excitation, the loss of the object, the loss of the object's love, and castration anxiety. In what is perhaps more poetic language, Winnicott (1974) briefly lists a number of primitive agonies, along with their characteristic defenses. These include a return to an unintegrated state, falling forever, loss of psychosomatic collusion, loss of sense of the real, and loss of capacity to relate to objects.

Sara struggled to put into words the feelings evoked during and after conflict with her mother. Gripped with fear that she might be abandoned forever, she described feeling that her "stomach might drop out" of her body. These feelings were so overwhelming that she often could not eat at school. Like Winnicott's poetic description of "falling forever," Sara is speaking to a repeated experience of sudden and unexpected loss of emotional connection with her mother. We can make use of our own imaginative capacities to better understand her experience. If you've ever been on a roller coaster, for example, you have a sense of what falling feels like. The hands tighten into fists, the back arches, and the stomach drops. In fact, we come into the world hardwired with something like a fear of falling. The Moro reflex, an infantile reflex normally present in all newborns, is a response to a sudden loss of support. Such an imaginative exercise serves to increase our ability to empathically immerse ourselves within Sara's emotional experience.

Psychic Skin

As previously described, Sara was subjected to intense physical and psychological intrusion. In her earliest weeks, during the very time she was most isolated from human, skin-to-skin contact, she was exposed to the endless examinations and surveillance of a neonatal intensive care unit. With family photographs from her time in the hospital, she reconstructed a narrative of endless penetration by syringe after syringe; when she talked about this aspect of her life, it evoked a visceral sense of what this period might have felt like for her.

Here, again, the analyst's imaginative capacities are essential to facilitating empathic immersion. Imagine, for a moment, that the body is a soft thing, filled with blood and bone and other life-giving processes that are remarkable for their intricacy and vulnerability. And in these earliest moments, for Sara that softness meant pain – physical and emotional – as her body was penetrated and damaged inside and out. The skin could not be relied upon as a barrier to keep her insides safe from the dangers of the environment, or even to keep her insides safely tucked inside. Moreover, the skin of a loving caretaker was not available as reinforcement. In these earliest years, this would have been both a deeply physical and psychological experience.

Discussing the role of skin in early development, Bick (1968) notes that the most primitive parts of the personality have no binding force of their own. They need a way to be held together, and the containing object, in the sense we have described in early chapters, that in optimal development is taken in as psychological structure over time will be experienced concretely as the skin that holds together all the parts of the self that depend upon it for coherence. In her incubator, without physical and emotional holding, Sara's skin received little emotional investment from her caretakers and she could not rely upon their help in managing the experiences that she was forced to endure. In this way, she came to experience herself as always having the potential to fall apart.

In a brief aside, Winnicott (1974) comments that the fear of falling forever is defended against by "self-holding." Bick (1968), with her notion of second-skin formations, was the first to describe one form that this self-holding might take. For Bick, second-skin formations are a defensive attempt – pseudo-independent forms of protection such as muscular tension or reliance upon particular sensory experiences – to provide self-cohesion. The patient's attempts at self-holding constitute a second-skin, which is a best attempt at holding the personality together.

Bick (1968) notes that this phenomenon is most easily studied in the relationship between analyst and patient in the context of problems of dependence and separation. In the following example, we can most clearly see the way that being thin served as a secondary skin for Sara. During treatment, she had increasingly been able to make use of the containment our relationship provided; this, in turn, made it possible for her to bear the intensity of her anxieties about falling apart without resorting to self-starvation. However, shortly before a planned vacation, she began to increase her food restriction once again. My vacation confronted her with her dependence upon me, which evoked past experiences of being left without emotional contact, as she was both in the incubator and, similarly, in her relationship with her mother. In this situation, she turned once again to self-starvation as an omnipotent means of managing overwhelming anxieties while also eschewing the pains of separation and loss associated with dependence upon me.

Here we must make an imaginative leap. How is it that the experience of being thin, of being intensely thin, might provide a kind of primitive physical and psychological holding? I imagine the progression as follows: first, the anxieties began to manifest as the fear and the feeling of becoming fat – of falling apart, a mess of loose skin, bulging stomach, flabby arms. Then Sara's caloric restriction countered this experience, giving her the feeling of being lean and compact – in essence, together once more. The experience of starvation – the intensity of its sensations – formed a hard physical shell that replaced the holding ordinarily provided by our relationship.

The Entropic Body

For Sara, my vacation was disastrous. We had established a support team for the period of my absence, but she lost almost 12 pounds in two weeks. When I returned, she greeted me with a cold and vacant stare that, over several days, transformed into a smoldering rage. I had anticipated that our time apart would be difficult for her, but I had not imagined that she would return to food restriction with such intensity. For several months, we discussed her fury at my betrayal and, over time, the sense of camaraderie that we had previously enjoyed began to return. And yet I sensed that part of her had not returned: that she, somehow, was not trusting me again. And in fact, she did not regain the pounds that she had lost but hovered steadily at her all-too-thin weight.

When I brought this up directly Sara said, "It's true. I hate to say it, but our relationship really can't compete with this. . . . It's reliable; it's under my control. It works." The experience of emaciation provided a kind of psychological holding that she desperately needed, without the risks of having to rely on another to provide it. In my view, this holding is provided through a particular defensive deployment of the body, as elaborated in Goldberg's (2004) model of the somatic false self. Goldberg's model describes how the body may be colonized and put to use for "false self" purposes, generating a façade of social appropriateness and functionality through auto-stimulation, auto-hypnosis, and alterations of consciousness, leaving the underlying vulnerable self in dissociated isolation. Patients with anorexia nervosa emaciate their bodies to create a physical experience that, similarly, masks an underlying self marked by profound vulnerability. This is the body-state that defines anorexia nervosa (Petrucelli, 2014).

Imagine the starving body. The hands and feet are frightfully cold and numb. The stomach and cheeks are concave, sunken in on themselves, and the protrusions of the ribs painful against thin and brittle skin. Not only is this startling to outside observers, but these physical changes are also palpable for patients themselves. Many patients report being able to feel their heartbeat even when they are physically at rest. A sort of deadening calm descends upon mind and body, flattening out all signs of living vitality. The ring of desire can be heard only in the faraway distance. Indeed, it has often been pointed out that significant weight loss elicits physiological adaptations that reduce arousal. With prolonged starvation, parasympathetic activation is increased (Miller, Redlich, & Steiner, 2003) and bradycardia often develops (Mitchell & Crow, 2006). These physiological adaptations reduce the overall intensity of affect (Craig, 2004) and mute hunger cues (Wang, Hung, & Randall, 2006).

This is the entropic body, the somatic state of maximal rest sought by anorexic patients. The search for the entropic body is an attempt to approximate the soothing functions that should have been internalized during separation-individuation in healthy development. In a successful treatment, the relationship between analyst and patient may provide some of these same comforting functions. It is our hope, of course, that the analytic relationship can facilitate the development of healthy pathways toward separation and individuation. And yet how can it compete with the entropic body, which is always available and albeit dangerous, so effective? It is a body-state (Petrucelli, 2014) that obviates the need for dependence upon another.

As our third year of treatment began, Sara said, "I see that there's more available to me when I'm connected to you, and to everyone else. But is it worth the cost? I still don't know for sure." We spent many months talking about this dilemma. It is difficult for a human relationship to compete with the omnipotently controlled safety and gratification provided by the entropic body, especially against a background of profound early trauma. The task is to maintain hope that the gratifications of relatedness are sufficient for her to increasingly relinquish her entropic body, while also remaining open to her profound disappointment in what relatedness can offer.

Sara has slowly put on some weight, though she has not yet reached the weight she had obtained before my absence. At present, she is an engaging and often profoundly insightful young woman who is preparing to enter college nearby so that she can remain in treatment with me. Her entropic body remains, in an attenuated form, a prominent body-state in her psychological and relational repertoire. And yet she also recognizes and values the pull of relatedness and all that it can offer, and this brings us both hope.

References

Bick, E. (1968). The experience of skin in early object-relations. *The International Journal of Psychoanalysis*, *49*, 484–486.

Bion, W. R. (1962). *Learning from experience*. London: Heinemann.

Craig, A. D. (2004). Human feelings: Why are some more aware than others? *Trends in Cognitive Sciences*, *8*, 239–241. https://doi.org/10.1016/j.tics.2004.04.004

Ferrari, A. B. (2004).4 *from the eclipse of the body to the dawn of thought*. London: Free Association Books.

Freud, S. (1926). Inhibitions, symptoms, and anxiety. In J. Strachey (Ed. & trans.), *The standard edition of the complete psychological works of Sigmund Freud* (Vol. 20, pp. 77–175). London: Hogarth Press.

Goldberg, P. (2004). Fabricated bodies: A model for the somatic false self. *International Journal of Psycho-Analysis*, *85*, 823–840. https://doi.org/10.1516/KFG7-97TU-EP99-1HR1

Grinberg, L. (1962). On a specific aspect of countertransference due to the patient's projective identification. *International Journal of Psychoanalysis*, *43*, 436–440.

Horner, A. J. (1980). The roots of anxiety, character structure, and psychoanalytic treatment. *Journal of American Academy of Psychoanalysis*, *8*, 565–573. https://doi.org/10.1521/jaap.1.1980.8.4.565

Kohut, H. (1977). *The restoration of the self*. New York, NY: International Universities Press.

Lombardi, R. (2009). Body, affect, thought: Reflections on the work of Matte Blanco and Ferrari. *The Psychoanalytic Quarterly*, *78*(1), 123–160.

Miller, S. P., Redlich, A. D., & Steiner, H. (2003). The stress response in anorexia nervosa. *Child Psychiatry & Human Development*, *33*, 295–306. https://doi.org/10.1023/A:1023036329399

Mitchell, J. E., & Crow, S. (2006). Medical complications in anorexia nervosa and bulimia nervosa. *Current Opinion in Psychiatry*, *19*, 438–443. https://doi.org/10.1097/01.yco.0000228768.79097.3e

Petrucelli, J. (Ed.). (2014). *Body-states: Interpersonal and relational perspectives on the treatment of eating disorders*. New York, NY: Routledge.

Shabad, P. (1993). Repetition and incomplete mourning: The intergenerational transmission of traumatic themes. *Psychoanalytic Psychology*, *10*(1), 61–75.

Wang, T., Hung, C. C., & Randall, D. J. (2006). The comparative physiology of food deprivation: From feast to famine. *Annual Review of Physiology*, *68*(1), 223–251. https://doi.org/10.1146/annurev.physiol.68.040104.105739

Williams, G. (1997). Reflections on some dynamics of eating disorders: "No entry" defenses and foreign bodies. *International Journal of Psychoanalysis*, *78*(5), 927–941.

Winnicott, D. W. (1974). Fear of breakdown. *International Review of Psycho-Analysis*, *1*, 103–107.

Wooldridge, T. (2018). The entropic body: Primitive anxieties and secondary skin formation in anorexia nervosa. *Psychoanalytic Dialogues*, *28*(2), 189–202.

Chapter 6

Gender, Culture, and Desire

Patients with eating disorders often struggle to tolerate desire, instead engaging in repeated and immediate action as a means of foreclosing the experience of wanting. We begin this chapter by examining the nature of desire. From one point of view, which begins with Freud, desires are already-formed inner strivings awaiting direction and growth, only secondarily shaped by the relational and cultural surround. With a post-modern, constructivist epistemology, on the other hand, desire is a function of its context and must find a "container of desire" (Brisman, 2002, p. 331) – a language provided first in important early relationships and, later, by the larger relational and cultural surround – for its expression. Desire cannot be understood apart from the contexts, relational and cultural, that shape it. A patient with bulimia, for example, may not desire food as a substitute for mother but, rather, because that is the only available "vocabulary" through which her desire can be expressed. The analyst's task becomes not only to uncover desires that have been defended against but also to help the patient begin to want freely so that, over time, new containers of desire can emerge, both inside and outside the analytic relationship.

The question of desire leads us to a consideration of female gender development. Gender differences are dramatic in the prevalence of some eating disorders, with, for example, far more females than males diagnosed with anorexia and bulimia (Stice & Bohon, 2012). Conversely, it is widely recognized that muscle dysmorphia afflicts more males than females (Olivardia, 2007). Although a cultural analysis helps to elucidate this difference, it fails to explain why females are more susceptible to certain cultural influences than their male

DOI: 10.4324/9781003016991-7

counterparts and vice versa. With this in mind, we draw upon contemporary psychoanalytic models of gender development to explore the relationship between gender identity and agency (that is, a sense of oneself as a subject who can want and act upon those wants). We highlight the necessity of developing a diverse gender "repertoire" (Elise, 1998) – a sense of oneself as both masculine and feminine in various ways – to counter problematic gender identifications.

The Problem of Desire

From an early age, "Alexa" understood that there were two possibilities in her family: she could be sexy or fat. Her mother and father conveyed, to a degree that reflected their own obsession with this dichotomy, that the former was her birthright – a state that would make her sexually desirable, certainly, but also more likable by friends, family, and employers – but that the latter would be her fate were she to lose control of her hunger. When we first met, she was thin while retaining her feminine curves, well-dressed, and profoundly dissociated as she struggled with the emotional fallout from an assault that occurred the previous year. As she walked to my office, she was terrified of men on the street who, seeing her "beautiful body," not only would desire her but might also violate her. As she described a childhood marked by humiliation, abused at the hands of her schoolmates and her parents, she told me not only about the assault but about her participation in dangerous sadomasochistic sexual practices with her boyfriend each night.

When Alexa was thin, she felt like a "sex goddess," as we came to describe it. Her all-encompassing desire was precisely to surrender herself to the hands of an all-powerful other. While this felt like a kind of power (her desirability lent her a measure of control), it also felt terrifyingly passive, for the experience of submission always carried the potential for violation, heightened ever more since the assault the previous year but ultimately stemming from her mother's dehumanizing use of aggression and shame throughout her childhood. Over the coming months, she gained weight through frenzied overeating: at first a little but, as the weeks passed, more quickly. Able to reflect upon her behavior but unable to control it, she described how the pounds brought her an excruciating mixture of relief and self-loathing. On the one hand, she no longer seemed to elicit as much attention from men on the street, which felt safer. On the other, she was disgusted by her body, as her "fat" elicited an attacking internal object that mirrored her mother's biting description of the change: lazy, childish, selfish, and greedy.

Kernberg (1995) observes that patients with anorexia tend toward sexual inhibition, whereas those with bulimia are more likely to enact sadomasochistic sexual interactions, especially when eating disturbances temporarily recede. While Alexa never intentionally vomited, to my knowledge, she would engage in extensive binge eating as her desire overwhelmed her, its aftermath leaving her awash in shame. The eating-disordered patient's relationship with food has all the marks of a clandestine love affair: anticipation, excitement, secrecy, disappointment, emptiness, and shame. And like many such patients, the breadth of Alexa's desire is highly circumscribed. As a thin "sex goddess," she is overwhelmed by the desire to masochistically submit to a tantalizing, abusive, other: a concrete situation mirrored by the structure of her internal object world. As she gains weight, her desire manifests as a voracious hunger, providing relief and safety from dangerous men but also leaving her feeling ashamed, her mother's words echoing in her mind. Conspicuously absent are other kinds of desires, such as the desire for comfort and tenderness, emotional connection, or understanding in the context of a trusted relationship.

In her essay, *Wanting*, Brisman (2002) eloquently unpacks the nature of desire. From one point of view, desires are cast as already-formed inner strivings awaiting direction and growth that are only secondarily shaped by their contexts. Here, the analyst's role is seen as examining and interpreting factors that thwart the unfolding of these inner strivings. "The goal," she writes, "is to loosen the roadblocks and let the traffic flow" (p. 331). Whether desire is seen, as in Freud's libido theory, as the manifestation of physiologically derived sexual drives, only secondarily directed toward objects by the ego's efforts to negotiate with cultural demands, or as a prewired potential for interaction with a particular object, most importantly the mother, in this paradigm we fundamentally know what we want, even if that wanting is obscure to our conscious minds.

When she was thin, Alexa told me repeatedly about the intensity of her desire for sex. In my clinical experience, I have never encountered a desire so voracious: she detailed spending hours with her boyfriend each day having sex, each encounter punctuated by a dozen or more orgasms. Over time, a pattern emerged in which she became erotically obsessed with powerful, unavailable men. Each man tormented her, tantalizing her with the possibility of emotional and sexual affirmation, always keeping consummation just out of reach. Psychoanalysts operating from an objectivist epistemology might understand her sexual desire as a displacement of her need for attachment with an emotionally available, affirming other. Sex, in this view, is secondary to a relational need that only needs to be uncovered. In our work together, Alexa and I found this view to be a fruitful and revealing approach to understanding her object relations.

With the advent of post-modernism and the shift toward constructivist epistemologies, this view has been challenged. Ghent (2001) writes that need (and, by extension we might argue, desire) is "nothing more than an organized motivational system" (p. 21) that is not value-laden or essentially object-driven. Rather, there is a state of needing, a formless and fluid craving, inherent in us all. The expression of a desire is shaped by its past and present relational and cultural contexts (Brisman, ibid.). These ideas have real implications for our patients with eating disorders. The intolerance of desires shuts down human growth and the analytic process more generally. When patients indulge in action, immediately and repeatedly, it is likely that their actions serve to foreclose desire, rather than allow for it to take shape and emerge from its inchoate ground.

As Brisman (2002) points out, Moulton (1972a, 1972b, 1977, 1985) observes the ways in which mothers give language to the internal worlds of their daughters. The words they choose may confine, direct, and narrow the shape that their daughters' desires take. Alexa grew up in a family in which two pathways of desire were outlined: the first, thinness and sexual submission, were esteemed but dangerous while the second, food, was comforting and safe yet shameful. These were the only two "containers of desire" (Brisman, ibid., p. 331) at her disposal. Our effort could not be only to uncover other, different desires and to clear away defenses so that those desires might find expression, for those desires may never have formed in the first place.

Our work, rather, was to ask, "What, in fact, would allow [Alexa] the safety to want freely, without holding an object of desire, any object of desire, too close to her chest?" (Brisman, 2002, p. 335). What would make it possible for her to want without finding immediate satisfaction, whether in food or in submission? Ultimately, my effort was toward providing a different context, one in which an interaction between us facilitated the emergence of a greater breadth of desire, regardless of whether any particular desire might find satisfaction. This was only possible when she tolerated the anxiety evoked by objects of desire that were not under her omnipotent control through the seductive power of her beauty or the out-of-control voraciousness of a binge. For several years, I tolerated my desire for such a change without satisfaction as we worked together to shift her sense of what it meant to be a woman who could have desires and act to fulfill them.

Gender and Agency

A cultural perspective has been invaluable in describing how social influences contribute to the dramatic gender differences in the prevalence of eating disorders. Eating disorders are more prevalent in industrialized cultures and certain eating disorders – anorexia and bulimia, for example – are more prevalent in females than in males, mirroring cross-cultural differences in the emphasis placed on thinness for women (Miller & Pumariega, 2001). These have become more common during the latter half of the twentieth century, a period during which women's magazines published more articles about weight loss and American icons of beauty became significantly thinner (Owen & Laurel-Seller, 2000). Yet a cultural analysis alone may not fully explain why women are more susceptible to certain cultural influences than their male counterparts. To address this question, we will draw upon contemporary psychoanalytic models of gender development. In discussing this, we will focus on the relationship between gender identity and agency (that is, a sense of oneself as a subject who can want and act upon those wants).

Alexa and I spent considerable time discussing what it means to be a woman who is capable of desire and acting to fulfill those desires, as opposed to a woman who submits to the desires of others or enacts her hungers in secret, always accompanied by shame. Schoen (2015) conceptualizes eating disorders as disorders of a gendered, agentic self: a man or a woman who wants and acts to fulfill those wants. For her, the disturbances in agency in eating disordered patients are inextricable from disturbances in gendered identifications. Such patients tend to be deeply conflicted about the meanings with which they have imbued gendered categories and desires. Their symptoms reflect this insofar as a certain type of body is seen as symbolizing a specific gendered identity and particular appetites symbolize specific gendered desires.

Women, in Schoen's (ibid.) view, tend to have greater developmental difficulty integrating agency into their gendered identity and are vulnerable to occupying the "un-agentic" side of gendered splitting. In this splitting, pleasure in activity is seen as masculine, whereas pleasure in passivity, feminine (Dimen, 1991). In many cases, women's sense of themselves as active may be gender-dystonic, in the same way that a man's fantasies of passivity may express a fear of being homosexual, which is associated with femininity. Similarly, our society fails to confirm and admire little girls' exhibitionism except in relation to their physical experience (Sands, 1989). Eating disordered patients often grow up in families that place an inordinate amount of importance upon bodily appearance, including weight, and focus upon particular parts of the body: protruding tummies, thunder thighs, and tree-trunk legs. We see these same pathogenic qualities in much of the advertising that is directed toward women and girls (Groesz, Levine, & Murnen, 2002).

Although self-starvation as manifest in anorexia nervosa is a deadly form of self-destruction, it is also a healthy expression of the desire to be autonomous (Charatan, 2015). It is, in other words, an attempt to preserve an experience of agency – of having desires and acting to fulfill those desires – in an environment that otherwise forecloses it. This is especially apparent in cases where an eating disorder develops around puberty as an expression of "maturity fears" in those patients with histories of sexual abuse. Here, sexuality and the body have become a stage for the imposition of the other's needs, desires, and control, leading to a "poisoning of desire" (Slavin & Pollock, 1997, p. 582). Alexa's binge eating, similarly, was an attempt to preserve a space in which she could express her desire protected from highly threatening gender-based identifications, which cast her into masochistic submission. While this creative adaptation allowed her to preserve her sanity, it also severely limited her relational repertoire (Ogden, 2005).

Alexa was devastated as her career accomplishments, which during the first years of treatment were considerable, were virtually ignored by her parents who, instead, quickly redirected their conversations toward the importance of weight loss – a sign of "true success." There was no emotional mirroring of her accomplishments, in contrast to the fact that her father's success was lovingly celebrated within the family. To counter this I often emphasized her accomplishments and suggested that they were an expression of – not in spite of – her gendered self. Yet her family's negation of her success – in fact, the shame they sought to elicit because of contemporaneous weight gain – made it difficult for her to acknowledge her own agency in this domain.

As Tyson (1982) clarifies, core gender identity, gender role, and sexual orientation are distinct. In contemporary psychoanalytic thinking, gender identity emerges from a complex matrix of same-sex and cross-sex parental identifications. More than the recognition of anatomical difference and identification as male or female, gender development encompasses the ways in which masculinity and femininity are elaborated with personal meanings through the same-sex and cross-sex mental representations of self and other (Harris, 1991; Benjamin, 1995). Centrally important in gender development is the establishment of a coherent, unified experience of gender identity without sacrificing a diverse gender "repertoire" (Elise, 1998): a sense of oneself as both masculine and feminine in a myriad of ways.

It is likely that the idealization process is more fraught for girls than for boys, especially during the oedipal period when children seek to idealize the same-sex parent and for that parent to delight in the child's gender-linked attributes (Sands, 1989). Girls growing up in contemporary society may lack, relative to boys, figures that can be idealized, especially within the family. Mothers struggle to manage multiple and often contradictory roles. Traumatically disappointed with the pathways available for idealization in the relational sphere, girls may look outside the realm of relatedness for solutions. Compulsive eating, for example, can represent an attempt "to replace the selfobject (and the transmuting internalization it provides) with food (and the activity of eating)" (Kohut, 2009, p. 20). Eating may, in other words, become an attempt to shore up an otherwise fragile sense of self. Similarly, food itself may serve the function of an idealized other, the object of a passionate love affair: soothing, perfect, and capable of solving all problems. For Alexa, mother was not a figure in whom she could idealize female agency. Being a woman meant submitting to the sexual desire of another, for this was the notion of femininity that she had found in a mother who had sacrificed her career in service of her husband's professional development and who labored to sculpt her own female body into a shape that was compelling to him.

As discussed in the previous section, Alexa did not grow up in a context in which her desire might take other shapes. There were only two "containers of desire" (Brisman, ibid, p. 331) at her disposal and, as an adult, she both lacked other modes of expression and was unable to tolerate the anxieties that dystonic desires would stimulate in her. As a woman, she had only one option: to be a "sex goddess." Yet another option *was* available, one in which she could give her hunger free reign in the realm of food and live in a body that felt sexless or, as her mother often said, "childlike." This was an adaptive, albeit emotionally painful, way of escaping the anxieties aroused by the sexualization forced upon her by her early environment. In her binge-eating episodes, we found a desperate attempt to altogether disavow a set of gendered identifications that foreclosed her agency and exposed her to anxiety-provoking sexualization.

What made it difficult for Alexa to integrate agency with her sense of herself as a woman? Goldner (2011) writes, "Where little girls operate from the gender premise, 'I am female like you, and thus we are bonded via sameness,' young boys deploy the opposite axiom, 'I am not female like you, and we are separated via difference'" (p. 161). Also making this point, Sands (1989) observes that girls, who need not go through such a pronounced dis-identification from their mothers as their male counterparts, are likely to remain more psychologically connected to their mothers than boys. This, in turn, means that a mother's investment in her daughter is more likely to emphasize narcissistic elements, to be based upon experiencing the daughter as an extension of herself. In families of eating-disordered patients, the narcissistic use of the daughter by the mother is often immediately striking. Throughout the literature the degree of enmeshment or symbiosis between mother and daughter is remarked upon. Daughters are torn between the urgings of their own developmental strivings and their need to meet their mothers' narcissistic needs. Symptoms may provide a facsimile of psychological separation from the mother insofar as, for example, the anorexic patient takes control of what comes into her (Bruch, 1973) and the bulimic actively repudiates her need for the mother through purging (Selvini-Palazzoli, 1978).

Moreover, for girls, "bonded via sameness" to their mothers, masculinity and agency are easily conflated and agency tends to be undermined by the way that girls inhibit their use of aggression in the service of separation and individuation for fear of damaging that all-important connection. Eating disorders, from this point of view, arise both from an exacerbation of normative development challenges in differentiation from the mother stemming from the mother's relating to her daughter to fulfill her own narcissistic needs and from negative associations to masculinity, especially its equation with destructive aggression. When eating disordered symptoms arise in men, Schoen (ibid.) writes, they may signal difficulty integrating dependency needs into a masculine identification. Sands (2003) notes that men are more likely to express disavowed needs and wants through projections onto others – witness the preponderance of compulsive sexual behaviors in men – whereas women are more likely to use their own bodies to contain disavowed desires. Consider, for example, the rigid "performance" (Butler, 1995) of masculinity in muscle dysmorphia, which often reflects the failure to fluidly integrate masculine and feminine identifications. Schoen (ibid.) makes an additional point that affliction with a so-called "feminine" disorder may reflect the shame-ridden disavowal of feminine identifications and desires.

Alexa's mother needed her daughter to be beautiful insofar as she felt this would confirm her own beauty. Every flaw in her daughter's appearance, conversely, exacerbated her mother's own insecurities about her gendered appearance and desirability. This narcissistic mode of relating made it extremely difficult for Alexa to develop a sense of herself as an agentic woman. She was terrified of mobilizing her aggression in service of separation and individuation for this might irreparably damage her tie to a figure with whom she was deeply identified or elicit her wrathful and shame-inducing retaliation. On the contrary, when faced with her mother's criticisms in reality or in her internal object world, she became childlike and apologetic. Though she was devastated by these attacks, our discussions of them often elicited laughter as she desperately attempted to circumvent the shame they evoked (Lewis, 1992). Yet over time, as she began to experiment with an expanded sense of herself as an agent, we found that self-assertion elicited a problematic identification with her father as a ruthless, dangerous figure who disregarded the desires of others in favor of his own (largely sexual) self-interests. One of her mother's most frequently voiced criticisms of her father, she now recalled for the first time, had been about this fact and the possibility of being ruthless like her father filled her with guilt.

It was not only the equation of femininity with masochistic submission and its accompanying vulnerability that made inhabiting a womanly body terrifying; it was, also, that the claiming of agency, and the aggression inherent in it, seemed an expression of destructive hatred, akin to her father's extramarital affairs. Around the time that the "Me Too" movement entered public consciousness, she began a session with an offhand remark. "Men," she said, "know what they want. And what they want, they take." This gender-based splitting – passive versus active, wanted versus wanting, object versus subject (Schoen, 2015) – was undoubtedly overdetermined, reflecting the dynamics in her family of origin, the trauma of her assault, the misogyny and patriarchy of our cultural surround, and an underlying truth about gendered developmental processes. At the level of her psychic reality, this splitting served to isolate contradictory feelings, projecting aggression outward where it could be located *solely* in men and, hence, fueled persecutory anxiety.

While the idea of inhabiting a feminine body, which for her entailed vulnerability to sexual violation, terrified Alexa, the possibility of claiming her desire *as her own* was equally abhorrent. With agency as the sole property of men, to claim it risked casting her as a perpetrator who would overlook the subjectivity of the other. To claim her own desire, sexual or otherwise, was an aggressive act. Up until this point, we had understood her binge eating as an expression of previously disavowed hunger, exploding into consciousness and enacted in a frenzy of consumption only to recede and leave shame in its wake. Now we could articulate that it was also a means of managing her disavowed rage, a theme that became an important part of our work.

References

Benjamin, J. (1995). Sameness and difference: Toward an "overinclusive" model of gender development. *Psychoanalytic Inquiry*, *15*(1), 125–142.

Brisman, J. (2002). Wanting. *Contemporary Psychoanalysis*, *38*(2), 329–343.

Bruch, H. (1973). *Eating disorders ed.* New York, NY: Basic Books.

Butler, J. (1995). Melancholy gender-refused identification. *Psychoanalytic Dialogues*, *5*, 165–180.

Charatan, D. L. (2015). "I won't grow up, never grow up, not me!": Anorexia nervosa and maturity fears revisited. In J. Petrucelli (Ed.), *Body-states: Interpersonal and relational perspectives on the treatment of eating disorders* (Psychoanalysis in a new key). New York, NY: Routledge.

Dimen, M. (1991). Deconstructing difference: Gender, splitting, and transitional space. *Psychoanalytic Dialogues*, *1*(3), 335–352.

Elise, D. (1998). Gender repertoire: Body, mind, and bisexuality. *Psychoanalytic Dialogues*, *8*(3), 353–371.

Ghent, E. (2001). *Wish, need, drive, motive in the light of dynamic systems theory*. Presented at New York University Postdoctoral Program in Psychotherapy and Psychoanalysis, New York City, January 27.

Goldner, V. (2011). Trans: Gender in free all. *Psychoanalytic Dialogues*, *21*(2), 159–171.

Groesz, L. M., Levine, M. P., & Murnen, S. K. (2002). The effect of experimental presentation of thin media images on body satisfaction: A meta-analytic review. *International Journal of Eating Disorders*, *31*(1), 1–16.

Harris, A. (1991). Gender as contradiction. *Psychoanalysis Dialogues*, *1*(2), 197–224.

Kernberg, O. F. (1995). Technical approach to eating disorders in patients with borderline personality organization. *The Annual of Psychoanalysis*, *23*, 33–48.

Kohut, H. (2009). *How does analysis cure?* Chicago, IL: University of Chicago Press.

Lewis, M. (1992). *Shame: The exposed self*. New York, NY: Free Press (1995).

Miller, M. N., & Pumariega, A. J. (2001). Culture and eating disorders: A historical and cross-cultural review. *Psychiatry: Interpersonal and Biological Processes*, *64*(2), 93–110.

Moulton, R. (1972a). Psychoanalytic reflections on women's liberation. *Contemporary Psychoanalysis*, *8*, 197–223.

Moulton, R. (1972b). Sexual conflicts of contemporary women. In E. G. Witenberg (Ed.), *Interpersonal explorations in psychoanalysis* (pp. 196–217). New York, NY: Basic Books.

Moulton, R. (1977). Women with double lives. *Contemporary Psychoanalysis*, *13*, 64–84.

Moulton, R. (1985). The effect of the mother on the success of the daughter. *Contemporary Psychoanalysis*, *21*, 266–283.

Ogden, T. H. (2005). What I would not part with. *Fort Da, 11*(2), 8–17.

Olivardia, R. (2007). Muscle dysmorphia: Characteristics, assessment, and treatment. In J. K. Thompson & G. Cafri (Eds.), *The muscular ideal: Psychological, social, and medical perspectives* (pp. 123–139). Washington, DC: American Psychological Association.

Owen, P. R., & Laurel-Seller, E. (2000). Weight and shape ideals: Thin is dangerously in. *Journal of Applied Social Psychology, 30*(5), 979–990.

Sands, S. (1989). Female development and eating disorders: A self psychological perspective. In A. Goldberg (Ed.), *Progress in self psychology* (Vol. 5, pp. 75–104). New York, NY: Analytic Press.

Sands, S. (2003). The subjugation of the body in eating disorders: A Particularly female solution. *Psychoanalytic Psychology, 20*(1), 103–116.

Schoen, S. (2015). "You're the one that I want": Appetite, agency, and the gendered self. In J. Petrucelli (Ed.), *Body-states: Interpersonal and relational perspectives on the treatment of eating disorders* (Psychoanalysis in a new key). New York, NY: Routledge.

Selvini-Palazzoli, M. (1978). *Self-starvation From individual to family therapy in the treatment of anorexia nervosa.* New York, NY: Jason Aronson.

Slavin, J. H., & Pollock, L. (1997). The poisoning of desire. *Contemporary Psychoanalysis, 33*, 573–593.

Stice, E., & Bohon, C. (2012). Eating disorders. In T. Beauchaine & S. Lindshaw (Eds.), *Child and adolescent psychopathology* (2nd ed.). New York, NY: Wiley.

Tyson, P. (1982). A developmental line of gender identity, gender role, and choice of love object. *Journal of the American Psychoanalytic Association, 30*, 61–86.

Chapter 7

Affect Regulation, Dissociation, and Body Imaginings

In this chapter, we begin with a discussion of a perspective from the relational school of psychoanalysis that regards the self not as a supraordinate and comprehensive structure, stable and consistent over time, but as decentralized and composed of relatively discrete psychic structures – "selves" – that, in a good enough developmental situation, attain an "illusion" of coherence and continuity (Bromberg, 1998). In this paradigm, *relational trauma* is defined as exposure to chronic misattunement and prolonged states of dysregulation in the context of an early attachment relationship. This leads to self-states becoming more or less dissociated. We use these ideas to formulate the notion of the "hungry self," a self-state prominent in patients with binge eating disorder like "Alexa," who was introduced in the previous chapter. With these ideas in mind, we consider how the experience of body image may vary according to the shifting landscape of dissociatively structured self-states. We focus on the way that body image is an expression of past relational experiences and how, in those patients with histories of relational trauma, an important aspect of treatment is helping patients to "stand in the spaces" (Bromberg, 1998) in order to understand the dynamics driving shifting experiences of body image. As these dynamics are increasingly put into words, patients' body images will likely gain greater stability.

Self-States, Affect Regulation, and Dissociation

It is fruitful to think of Alexa, discussed in the previous chapter, as occupying two different self-states: the first metaphorically expressed

DOI: 10.4324/9781003016991-8

by her thin, attractive body, in which she experiences herself as a "sex goddess" whose all-encompassing desire is to surrender herself to the hands of an all-powerful other, and the second expressed by weight gain that leaves her feeling "sexless." In each of these self-states, she experiences herself as a significantly different kind of person, with different thoughts, feelings, and behaviors. Over the past few decades, a prominent line of relational theorizing (e.g., Bromberg, 1998; Davies, 1996) has emerged that regards the self not as a unitary, over-arching structure, mostly stable and consistent over time, but as decentralized and composed of relatively discrete psychic structures – "selves" – that, in a good enough developmental situation, attain an "illusion" of coherence and continuity (Bromberg, 1998). Each self-state comprises ways of thinking, feeling, and acting – different ways of being in different contexts. In a sense, each self-state is its own personality system, an assemblage of affective and cognitive processes that make up "versions" of us (Hill, 2015).

In optimal development, the self-state system is integrated. Our various self-states are compatible with one another and we shift fluidly between them, retaining a feeling of relative coherence and unity among different versions of ourselves (Hill, 2015). Some self-states, however, may be partially or fully dissociated. These self-states are activated involuntarily and automatically, coming upon us without warning. We are typically unaware that we are in a partially dissociated self-state, for in these states we know that we are different but have only a shallow understanding of what is happening to us (ibid.). We may remember other ways of being ourselves, but they feel distant and foreign. While Alexa could remember her behaviors, and many of her thoughts and feelings, across self-states, there was very little capacity to "stand in the spaces" (Bromberg, 1998) and reflect upon the dynamics that ordered their shifting landscape.

Central to the self-state paradigm is affect regulation theory. Affect may be divided into primary and categorical, or discrete, affect. The former is the somatic representation of the state of the organism, a sensorimotor physiological representation that generates a felt sense (Hill, 2015). It is the nonverbal representation of the body. Categorical affects, on the other hand, are what we typically call emotions, such as the seven delineated by Darwin (1872/1965): shame, sadness, joy, anger, surprise, fear, and disgust. Both primary and categorical affect comprise the experiential-cognitive appraisal system that tells us what things mean to us and what our motives, needs, and desires are. The capacity to regulate affect emerges from the early attachment relationship, a time when children are crucially dependent upon their caretakers for self-regulation. Growth-enhancing experience relies upon the attachment figure's attunement, established via implicit communication between attachment figure and infant. Siegel (1999) describes how attunement allows the parent to help the infant to organize its own mind. The regulation of the infant's affect by the attachment figure – a process called dyadic regulation – occurs at first largely through touch and, over time, through nonverbal, implicit communications of affect: "touch at a distance" (Hill, ibid., p. 10). In optimal development, we can alternate between auto- and dyadic regulation as necessary, depending on our needs and capacities at a given developmental stage. Later in development, a secondary affect regulation system emerges – mentalization (Fonagy, 1999; Allen & Fonagy, 2006) – that consists of verbal-reflective, slow, deliberate, conscious cognitive processes (Hill, ibid.). Mentalization, a different concept than mentalisation described in *Chapter 1: Alexithymia and the Psychic Elaboration of Emotion*, is the capacity to understand ourselves and others as having mental states, thus comprehending our own and other's intentions and affects.

In this paradigm, *relational trauma*, which can be defined as exposure to chronic misattunement and prolonged states of dysregulation in the context of the early attachment relationship, is seen as undermining the capacity for affect regulation. In contrast to the "complex" or "developmental" trauma described by Herman (1997) and van der Kolk (2005), which focuses on sexual, physical, and verbal abuse and neglect within the attachment relationship, relational trauma points to the less obvious, and in fact often invisible, trauma that occurs within the attachment relationship. When seeking affect regulation from the attachment figure, the child encounters responses that exacerbate, rather than modulate, her emotional dysregulation. The stressor is the relationship itself, hence the term relational trauma. In the face of relational trauma, self-states may become more or less dissociated and, given the resulting impaired capacity for affect regulation, dissociation likely becomes a chronic pattern of defense.

Although the meaning of the term *dissociation* varies among analytic thinkers, Hill (2015) proposes that dissociated self-states share three characteristics: automaticity, compartmentalization, and altered states of consciousness. Dissociated self-states are *automated* in that they are activated involuntarily and involve scripted behavioral and psychological responses. They are *compartmentalized* because their content is involuntarily isolated. Commonly, aspects of the traumatic event cannot be voluntarily remembered, assessed, and integrated into one's overall functioning. In extreme cases, an entire personality system, including memories, sense of self, and representational and perceptual dispositions, are segregated and kept from consciousness in other self-states. And finally, trauma-based *altered states of consciousness* may generate a sense of detachment. We feel out of touch with our body-based feelings and emotionally distant from others and, in extreme cases, we may feel ourselves to be out of our bodies entirely.

There is considerable empirical evidence that dissociation is prominent in patients with eating disorders. There is, for example, substantial empirical literature documenting the association between binge eating disorder and childhood maltreatment (Amianto et al., 2018; Imperatori et al., 2016; Allison, Grilo, Masheb, & Stunkard, 2007; Grilo & Masheb, 2001). In one study, for example, 83% of BED patients reported some form of childhood maltreatment, with 59% reporting emotional abuse, 36% physical abuse, 30% sexual abuse, 69% emotional neglect, and 49% physical neglect. Emotional abuse was significantly associated with greater body dissatisfaction, higher depression, and lower self-esteem in both men and women (Grilo & Masheb, 2001). In another study, subliminal threat cues increased state dissociation (particularly levels of derealization) in bulimic women but had no effect on the nonclinical group, seeming to support the idea that bulimic women are more vulnerable to dissociation in response to specific threats (i.e., state dissociation) (Hallings-Pott, Waller, Watson, & Scragg, 2005). In a third, difficulties with affect regulation and dissociation were found to be significant mediators between childhood traumas and eating psychopathology (Moulton, Newman, Power, Swanson, & Day, 2015).

From a psychoanalytic point of view, Bromberg (2001) suggests that eating disorders develop as the result of a prolonged necessity in infancy to control trauma and affect dysregulation, leading to a mental structure that has been shaped by dissociative dynamics and an impaired faith in human relatedness. Eating disordered symptoms represent the "repackaging" of unlinked states of mind into symptomatic thoughts, feelings, and behaviors – dissociated self-states. These dissociative defenses inevitably manifest in the transference as well, representing the patient's attempt to "stay enough in relationship with the human environment to survive the present while, at the same time, keeping the needs for more intimate relatedness sequestered but alive" (Sands, 1994, p. 149).

Binge Eating Disorder: The "Hungry Self"

To illustrate how these ideas might apply to patients with eating disorders, we will discuss a self-state commonly encountered by patients with binge eating disorder, which might be referred to as the "hungry self." Many of these patients, like Alexa, describe a primary relationship, often with a mother, who they experienced as either emotionally fragile or grandiose. In the history that emerges, the narcissistic aspects of the mother's character appear to contribute to a dynamic in which the child's emotional needs were largely unacknowledged, much less appropriately satisfied. In other words, the mother's narcissistic vulnerabilities made it difficult for her to experience the child as a separate person with her own needs and desires, which would be a pre-requisite for responding to them appropriately. Alexa's mother, for example, was strongly invested in her daughter's beauty and sexuality, for to have a beautiful daughter bolstered her own self-esteem. Her need for her daughter to be beautiful was so powerful that she could not assess the impact of this upon her developing child. Against this backdrop, Alexa experienced her mother as unreceptive to the communication of her own emotional longings, needs, and desires, constituting a breakdown in containment as discussed in *Chapter 3: Early Relationships, Object Relations, and Traumatic Themes*. In the face of this traumatic theme, she developed a profound "hunger" for emotional nourishment, particularly from her mother, and accompanying frustrated rage at the deprivation that she was forced to endure.

By the time she became an adult, this "hungry self" had been cordoned off so that it only emerges when the dissociative defensive structure fails, as a binge eating episode, which concretely expresses her hunger for nourishment and rage at its frustration.

When the "hungry self" – a combination of need and rage – emerges in a binge episode, the patient's thinking and perception is dissociatively narrowed. She becomes absorbed in the movements and sensations – not the meaning – of eating and is unable to evaluate that eating against norms grounded in reality such as, for example, what might constitute an appropriately sized meal or a healthy selection of food to eat (Tibon & Rothschild, 2009). Alexa described experiences of becoming so immersed in the experience of eating that only when she "awoke," hours later, could she recognize the enormous amount of food that she had consumed. The sole feeling she could recall was a persistent, though subtle, feeling of shame that accompanied her as she ate. In my experience, patients with binge eating disorder exist on a continuum, with some having no awareness, intellectual or emotional, of their profound feelings of need and rage with others having a much greater awareness of these feelings but not yet having found a relational context that would facilitate a fuller integration of them. Both, to varying degrees, make use of binge eating as a channel through which to express these feelings, which remain more-or-less dissociated from their conscious minds in their day-to-day lives

Body Image and Body Imaginings

In the *Image and Appearance of the Human Body* (1950), psychoanalyst Paul Schilder began to think about the bodily experience from a psychological and sociological point of view. In the past, research had focused upon distortions in body perception caused by brain damage. In contrast, Schilder defines *body image* as the meanings and fantasies about our bodies that we form in our own minds. Hoffer (1950) suggests that by the second year of life an infant has an oral-tactile concept of his own body. Over time, this becomes a relatively stable body image. Although not identical with the actual bodily configuration, in health body image is more-or-less congruent with it. Yet clinicians who work with eating disorders can attest to the often-dramatic fluctuations in body image that afflict these patients. In this section, we will discuss how body image is a relationally constituted phenomenon, fluctuating as relational identifications shift for the patient. Put differently, body image may vary as self-states vary, with each self-state bringing to the foreground relational identifications that, in turn, shape the way that the body is experienced.

In normal development, a child acquires a sense of himself as both lovable and attractive through early, preverbal interactions. The first exchanges between the mother and baby are intensely physical. The preverbal interplay between mother and baby – an intricately patterned communication of pain and pleasure, excitement and relaxation – lays the foundation of the child's developing sense of self. As Lemma (2009) points out, visual interactions play a significant part in this dance. Psychoanalytic studies of blind children suggest that sight plays a primary role in the child's earliest "taking in" of important relationships, leading to structure building and ego differentiation (Sandler, 1963; Fraiberg & Freedman, 1964). Indeed, the mother's face is the child's first emotional mirror (Winnicott, 1967), insofar as it reflects back to him aspects of his own emotional experience. In healthy development, the mother's loving gaze takes in and receives the child, and this gaze serves as the beginning of an intact body image, which is further consolidated over time. Ultimately, the child's internal representations of his own body are impacted not only by his (objective) physical differences but also by the relationally constellated meanings that are ascribed to those physical differences. Recognizing this fact, Lemma (2009) proposes the term "body imagining(s)" to highlight the fluid, fantasy-based nature of our internal representations of the body formed by the self in interaction with the other.

The idea of body imaginings (Lemma, ibid.) allows us to begin to think about how patients experience their bodies differently – sometimes large or small, powerful or weak – in relation to the analyst at various points in treatment. With this idea, we recognize that body image is not fixed. For example, an (objectively) small body can be experienced as powerful and dangerous or weak and shameful, depending on the internal representations active at any given time. Importantly, patients with eating disorders often present with body imaginings that are segregated into different self-states. In Alexa's "hungry self" self-state, she loathed her body, focusing particularly on the rolls of fat around her stomach and the excess flesh of her thighs. To be fat, she said, was to be "lazy, childish, selfish, and greedy," a description that mirrored her mother's complaints about her throughout her childhood. One of the aspects of relational trauma, which contributes to the emotional dysregulation that drives dissociation and, over time, the segregation of different self-states, is shame experienced at the hands of an attachment figure. Alexa's shame was intolerable, for it threatened her fragile self with collapse, and at an early age, she sought ways to dissociatively numb this feeling. In one session, she described pinching the skin on her arms to a degree that required stitches and antibiotics to stave off infection. This self-harm, we discovered, allowed her to distance herself from the painful feelings of shame that she could not regulate on her own. The shame reflected an experience of being "seen" as defective and unlovable which could not be elaborated into words and images and so remained concretely experienced as a body imagining.

Although Alexa's body was, in fact, physically larger when she was engaged in binge eating, more important from a psychoanalytic point of view is how she *experienced* her body in the self-state that gave rise to binge eating. We can see this, for example, in how she recalls her mother's complaint that she is "lazy, childish, selfish, and greedy." This stands in contrast to her experience at other times, when she experiences her body as irresistible to those around her, a body imagining (Lemma, 2009) corresponding with her parents' sexualization of her throughout her childhood. Although her weight gain made it difficult for her to see that her feelings about her body were linked to more than the concrete reality of her weight, as her weight stabilized later in treatment it became more apparent that her sense of her body varied dramatically, often independently of whether she had gained or lost weight. We were able to understand her shifting body image as a way of "remembering" early relational experiences, revived in a given moment because of what was transpiring in the transference-countertransference between us, and, eventually, the instability of her body image ameliorated as her capacity to articulate her emotional experience strengthened.

References

Allen, J., & Fonagy, P. (Eds.). (2006). *Handbook of mentalization-based treatment*. Chichester, UK: Wiley.

Allison, K. C., Grilo, C. M., Masheb, R. M., & Stunkard, A. J. (2007). High self-reported rates of neglect and emotional abuse, by persons with binge eating disorder and night eating syndrome. *Behaviour Research and Therapy*, *45*(12), 2874–2883.

Amianto, F., Spalatro, A. V., Rainis, M., Andriulli, C., Lavagnino, L., Abbate-Daga, G., & Fassino, S. (2018). Childhood emotional abuse and neglect in obese patients with and without binge eating disorder: Personality and psychopathology correlates in adulthood. *Psychiatry Research*, *269*, 692–699.

Bromberg, P. M. (1998). *Standing in the spaces: Essays on clinical process, trauma, and dissociation*. Hillsdale, NJ: Analytic Press.

Bromberg, P. M. (2001). Treating patients with symptoms – and symptoms with patience: Reflections on shame, dissociation, and eating disorders. *Psychoanalytic Dialogues*, *11*(6), 891–912.

Darwin, C. (1965). *The expression of the emotions in man and animals*. Chicago: University of Chicago Press (Original work published 1872).

Davies, J. M. (1996). Linking the "Pre-Analytic" with the postclassical: Integration, dissociation, and the multiplicity of unconscious process. *Contemporary Psychoanalysis*, *32*, 553–576.

Fonagy, P. (1999). Attachment, the development of the self, and its pathology in personality. In J. Derksen et al. (Eds.), *Treatment of personality disorder* (pp. 53–68). New York, NY: Plenum.

Fraiberg, S. H., & Freedman, D. A. (1964). Studies in the ego development of the congenitally blind child. *Psychoanalytic Study of the Child*, *19*, 113–169.

Grilo, C. M., & Masheb, R. M. (2001). Childhood psychological, physical, and sexual maltreatment in outpatients with binge eating disorder: Frequency and associations with gender, obesity, and eating-related psychopathology. *Obesity Research*, *9*(5), 320–325.

Hallings-Pott, C., Waller, G., Watson, D., & Scragg, P. (2005). State dissociation in bulimic eating disorders: An experimental study. *International Journal of Eating Disorders*, *38*(1), 37–41.

Herman, J. (1997). *Trauma and recovery: The aftermath of violence – from domestic abuse to political terror*. Guilford: New York.

Hill, D. (2015). *Affect regulation theory: A clinical model*. New York, NY: W. W. Norton.

Hoffer, W. (1950). Development of the body ego. *The Psychoanalytic Study of the Child*, *5*, 18–23.

Imperatori, C., Innamorati, M., Lamis, D. A., Farina, B., Pompili, M., Contardi, A., & Fabbricatore, M. (2016). Childhood trauma in obese and overweight women with food addiction and clinical-level of binge eating. *Child Abuse & Neglect*, *58*, 180–190.

Lemma, A. (2009). Being seen or being watched? A psychoanalytic perspective on body dysmorphia. *International Journal of Psychoanalysis*, *90*, 753–771.

Moulton, S. J., Newman, E., Power, K., Swanson, V., & Day, K. (2015). Childhood trauma and eating psychopathology: A mediating role for dissociation and emotion dysregulation? *Child Abuse & Neglect*, *39*, 167–174.

Sandler, A. M. (1963). Aspects of passivity and ego development in the blind infant. *Psychoanalytic Study of the Child*, *18*, 343–360.

Sands, S. H. (1994). What is dissociated? *Dissociation*, *7*, 145–152.

Schilder, P. (1950). *The image and appearance of the human body: Studies in the constructive energies of the psyche*. New York, NY: International Universities Press, Inc.

Siegel, D. (1999). *The developing mind: How relationship and the brain interact to shape who we are*. New York, NY: Guilford.

Tibon, S., & Rothschild, L. (2009). Dissociative states in eating disorders: An empirical Rorschach study. *Psychoanalytic Psychology*, *26*(1), 69.

Van der Kolk, B. H. (2005). Developmental trauma disorder: Towards a rational diagnosis for chronically traumatized children. *Psychiatric Annals*, *35*(5), 401–408.

Winnicott, D. W. (1967). The location of cultural experience. *International Journal of Psychoanalysis*, *48*, 368–372.

Chapter 8

The Role of the Father and the Paternal Function

This chapter will discuss the role of the father and of the paternal function – a term to be defined in the next paragraph – in patients with eating disorders. To make these ideas concrete, we will focus specifically on male patients with anorexia nervosa and muscle dysmorphia. One purpose served by the paternal function is to assist the child in separation and individuation from his mother. Through a father's establishing a loving bond with his son, his "attractive function" encourages the child's capacity to explore the outside world (Abelin, 1971). In the families of children who develop anorexia nervosa, the mother's use of the child to maintain her own equilibrium makes separation and individuation more difficult. In such families, a potentially important factor in whether the child goes on to develop anorexia nervosa is the strength of the paternal function, which optimally helps the child learn how to appropriately deploy his aggression in the service of separation and individuation. In these families, however, the relative absence of the paternal function may lead the anorexic-to-be to locate his experience of agency in relation to eating and his body, which he rigidly controls. In families of children who develop muscle dysmorphia, in contrast, the father may maintain his own equilibrium by keeping his son small, vulnerable, and weak. Whereas in optimal development the paternal function would facilitate the developing boy's separation and individuation, in these cases it instead threatens the child with the possibility of remaining forever lost in dependency upon his mother. To avoid this, the child defensively idealizes a particular form of masculinity characterized by "bigness" (Corbett, 2001)

DOI: 10.4324/9781003016991-9

that the paternal function comes to represent and that is concretely expressed by his drive for muscularity.

At the beginning of this chapter, it seems important to say a few words about the term *paternal function*. There is a long history of debate within psychoanalysis about sex and gender roles. As Davies and Eagle (2013) point out, one approach is to begin with the assumption that there are a set of functions that need to be performed by parents in the service of their child's emotional and physical development. To theorize these functions, we may assume that they consist of both maternal functions, those typically performed by the woman/ mother, and paternal functions, those typically performed by the man/ father. Within the literature, they suggest, the terms *maternal* and *paternal* – instead of *mother* and *father* – may have arisen to suggest that such functions may be performed by caretakers who are not necessarily the biological or even adoptive parents of the child. Yet they still retain strongly gendered associations and, as such, may unintentionally contribute to the marginalization of differently configured families.

Indeed, the diversity of present-day parenting arrangements makes clear that the paternal function is *not* necessarily provided by the male-sexed father. As Diamond (2017a, 2017b) points out, females, including the mother, often carry aspects of the paternal function and given the complexity of the paternal function, it cannot be "reduced to the empirical presence of the 'father'" (Perelberg, 2013, p. 581). In writing this chapter, I have experimented with using a nongendered term in lieu of paternal function, such as third-party function, as suggested by Fiorini (2013). In the end and with considerable ambivalence, I decided to retain gendered terminology because I wish to draw our attention to the existence of common gender pathways, masculine and feminine, in the development of both anorexia nervosa and muscle dysmorphia.

Mothers and Fathers in Anorexia Nervosa

As mentioned in earlier chapters, Hilde Bruch's (1962, 1973, 1978) foundational work was the first to describe anorexia nervosa in the language of object relations. In her view, self-starvation represents a struggle for autonomy, mastery, and self-esteem. Disturbances in the early mother–child relationship predispose the child to develop the disorder during adolescence, a time that demands an increased capacity for autonomous functioning. In her clinical work, she described over-involved mothers who appear to be domineering, intrusive, and discouraging of separation and individuation. This, she argued, creates an internal confusion in children, expressed through body image disturbance (overestimating their body size), interoceptive disturbance (an inability to identify and respond to internal sensations, including hunger, fullness, and affective states), and all-pervasive feelings of ineffectiveness and loss of control.

Since this seminal contribution, the literature on anorexia nervosa consistently points to disruptions in the mother–child relationship, describing intrusive mothers who struggle to facilitate separation and individuation, (Selvini Palazzoli, 1974), impose their wishes upon their children, forcing them into passive submission (Sours, 1974), and confront them with an "all-consuming, insatiable demand" to be needed (Hamburg, 1999). In the face of these dynamics, the anorexic child is cast as struggling with intense rage toward her mother, which is displaced onto her own body (Ritvo, 1976). As Zerbe (1993) writes, the refusal of food is "an autonomous statement, *par excellence*: "I don't need you. I don't need anything. I don't even need food to survive. I am totally independent" (p. 95). Chasseguet-Smirgel (1993, 1995) suggests that anorexic patients function on the level of unconscious fantasy in an autarchical manner. Lawrence (2001) casts anorexia as a manic defense, an effort to control an internal representation of the mother, and suggests that the bodily damage inflicted by the patient reflects the violence that is felt to be done to the internal mother.

In these formulations, the father is usually described as passive, absent, or otherwise unavailable to disrupt the symbiosis between mother and child (Hamburg, 1999; Sours, 1974; Zerbe, 1993). Beresin, Gordon, and Herzog (1989) interviewed 13 former patients with anorexia nervosa who described their mothers as intrusive, over-involved, concerned with appearance, and lacking in attunement to their children's needs, consistent with the theories just described, and their fathers as distant, successful, and over-involved with work to the neglect of their families. Similarly, Elliot (2010) interviewed 11 patients in the recovery process who described their fathers as unreliable and intermittently available. In both these studies, those interviewed seemed to feel a strong adherence to parental demands, disavowing a desire for independence and unprepared for adolescence, and a strong pressure to control their own needs, at times in an effort to protect their parents' marriages from the impact of those needs were they expressed.

Consider, in this vein, "Damien," a nearly 40-year-old patient who has struggled with anorexia nervosa since his teenage years. Early on, he tells me how the "terrible disease" has trapped him in perpetual dependence upon his parents, both financial and emotional, and has destroyed his physical health. As the analysis unfolds, I learn about his relationship to his mother, who he has always experienced as engulfing and intrusive, and with his father, who he experiences as distant and uninvolved, absorbed in his obsessional tendencies which manifest in compulsive hoarding behaviors. As a child, his mother would recruit him to provide "shoulder massages" in which she would remove her shirt and, covered only by her undergarments, insist that he minister to her pain. He describes many rooms of their large family home filled to the ceiling with receipts, papers, and books. He reveals how as a child, his father would often disappear from both mother and son for days as he retreated into his study to pursue these interests. This fueled his mother's disparagement of his father and her further emotional entanglement with her son.

Anorexia Nervosa and Agency

What has been lost to Damien, or at least significantly diminished, is his agency, in the sense that was described in *Chapter 3: Traumatic Themes, Repetition, and Mourning*. He is trapped in a closed sado-masochistic system with each instance of victimization motivating sadistic retaliation against his mother, manifesting in displacement as starvation and injury inflicted upon his own body. This leads to profound guilt, defended against by further victimization (Novick & Novick, 2016). His father, compromised in his own right, is unable to shield his son from his mother's engulfing attention or to assist him in developing a sense of autonomous identity. As this vignette suggests, agency and its derailments in patients with eating disorders may be the most encompassing perspective we have of these complex and multi-faceted illnesses to date, speaking to many aspects of the struggles that we encounter clinically (Zerbe, personal communication).

Little has been written about the relationship between anorexia nervosa and agency. Bruch (1962, 1973, 1978), with her usual foresight, identified a paralyzing sense of ineffectiveness and helplessness as characteristic of this population. In the empirical literature, Bers and Quinlan (1992) compared inpatients with anorexia nervosa to both control inpatients and non-patient controls on a measure of "ineffectiveness": a lack of appreciation of their own resources and confidence in their initiative, an inability to recognize their accomplishments and capabilities, and a feeling that they are not competent to lead a life of their own. Patients with anorexia nervosa and non-patient controls were differentiated in that the former showed a high interest in various activities and a low perceived ability in these activities, a "perceived-competence deficit." In short, the experience of agency in these patients was highly compromised. Feeling helpless and ineffective, they do not *experience* themselves as agents, capable of mobilizing their aggression to push up against the world. Ironically, clinicians, family members, and friends regularly experience these patients as having a profound impact on them.

To elaborate upon these findings, Bers, Blatt, and Dolinsky (2004) examined the sense of self of patients with anorexia nervosa by obtaining open-ended self-descriptions of 77 women between the ages of 14 and 24, with groups of psychiatric patients with anorexia nervosa (n = 15), control psychiatric patients (n = 15), and control non-patients (n = 48). Their self-descriptions were rated on 18 scales and fell into four factors (Agency, Reflectivity, Differentiation, and Relatedness) and two affective scales (Anxiety and Depression). The patient groups were distinguished from the non-patient group by a lower sense of Agency and Relatedness. The anorexia group was distinguished from the psychiatric patient group by the presence of heightened and harsh self-reflectivity. Surprisingly, physical descriptors and an external focus did not dominate these patients' self-descriptions. On the contrary, evident in their inner lives was intense self-scrutiny accompanied by endless self-loathing and self-criticism.

Paternal Function in Anorexia Nervosa

The paternal function plays an important role in facilitating the child's capacity to make use of his aggression. When aggression can be constructively harnessed, it contributes to an experience of the self as active and capable of having an impact upon one's internal and external worlds. It animates our efforts to "push up" and "push back" against the environment and against forces within us, lending our experience agency and empowerment. Through exerting an impact upon our environment that, by its nature, resists that impact to some degree, the child develops a sense of himself as causing or generating an action (Knox, 2011). Aggression, likewise, energizes the child's efforts to separate and individuate from his mother and to explore the outside world.

Herzog (1982, 1988, 2001, 2004, 2010) argues, based on his clinical observations, that a father's careful use of his own aggression, as part of his paternal function, consolidates a child's sense of himself and the management of his aggressive drive. In Herzog's (2004) paradigm, the paternal function is especially important in helping young boys – who likely have a greater aggressive endowment from birth (Archer, 2004) – learn to modulate their aggressive urges, especially during early development. Referencing his clinical work, he describes a painful emotional state, *father hunger*, which manifests in the absence of the father, actual or symbolic, and suggests that young boys' aggression may be amplified because the father's absence is perceived simultaneously as the child's own doing and as depriving the child of desperately needed protection. Boys, then, crucially depend on a father's guidance in the management of their aggression. This need to be "shown how" (Herzog, 2001) is a hallmark of their development.

There are good reasons for thinking that young girls also rely on the paternal function for assistance in developing the capacity to regulate their aggression. Girls tend to have greater difficulty integrating the experience of agency into their gendered identity and are vulnerable to occupying the "un-agentic" side of gendered splitting (Schoen, 2015). In this splitting, pleasure in activity is seen as masculine, whereas pleasure in passivity is seen as feminine (Dimen, 1991). In many cases, a woman's sense of herself as active may be gender-dystonic, in the same way that a man's fantasies of passivity may express a fear of being homosexual, which is associated with femininity. The integration of identification with the paternal object into a diverse gender "repertoire" (Elise, 1998) is central in the overcoming of this splitting so that aggression can be deployed in the service of agentic experience, and separation and individuation for both sexes. Writing about the prevalence of father hunger in anorexia, Maine (1991) describes the painful longing for the father, and his paternal function, frequently observed in female patients.

Muscle Dysmorphia and Gender Development

The main feature of muscle dysmorphia is body dissatisfaction (Olivardia, Pope, & Hudson, 2000), which often leads to the use of anabolic steroids and other physique-enhancing drugs and supplements, strictly controlled dietary plans, excessive exercise, and body "checking" behaviors. Many of those afflicted are drawn to bodybuilding to achieve the lean, hypertrophic, and muscular physique they desire. Those with muscle dysmorphia experience profound shame and embarrassment about their bodies. In addition, they often have a history of disordered eating (Olivardia, 2001) that involves contradictory strategies such as highly regimented diets to increase weight and muscularity while simultaneously engaging in purging behaviors or laxative use to avoid fat increase (Cafri et al., 2005; Choi, Pope, & Olivardia, 2002; Hildebrandt, Schlundt, Langenbucher, & Chung, 2006).

Although more research is needed to clarify the extent of the gender difference in muscle dysmorphia, it is widely recognized that it affects significantly more men than women (Olivardia, 2007, p. 131). Empirical research on body image disorders in women suggests that women, especially women with eating disorders, judge their bodies to be too large and aspire to often unrealistic levels of thinness (Cash & Pruzinsky, 2002; Garner, Garfinkel, Schwartz, & Thompson, 1980). Although there are fewer studies examining body image issues in men and boys, a growing body of research shows that males tend to desire a leaner and more muscular body. This preference for a muscular physique is already apparent in boys as young as six (Jacobi & Cash, 1994; Ricciardelli, McCabe, & Banfield, 2000).

Given the fact that muscle dysmorphia affects significantly more males than females, gender development may be implicated in the disorder. As many theorists have pointed out, the concepts of masculinity and femininity should not be understood as unitary. With this in mind, muscle dysmorphia may commonly express a particular masculine ideal in its extreme form. For Corbett (2001), this ideal involves "the wish and effort to be a big winner, not a small loser" (p. 6). The emotional experience of smallness and vulnerability is defended against by "an insistent, illusory display of bigness and agency" (p. 6). For Elise (2001), this is a "fortress of emotional self-sufficiency" – a citadel – that forecloses dependency and vulnerability. As Elise (ibid) remarks, this ideal, far from describing every man instead elaborates a myth of masculinity that men have to contend with even if it does not reflect their individual personalities. The pursuit of this ideal is an attempt to protect a vulnerable sense of self and disavows feelings of dependence, need, and vulnerability. This leads to increasing idealization of masculine attributes in an effort to avoid emotional experiences of weakness and vulnerability (Brady, 2017). This "burden of unrelenting bigness" (Brady, ibid., p. 198) constructs a version of masculinity that is an unachievable ideal.

Consider "John," an adolescent boy who attends treatment at the insistence of his mother after she found performance-enhancing supplements in his bedroom. In our first session – a family interview – his father, who works in the military, speaks with a hard edge and, in one interaction, seems to intimidate his son. His mother, in contrast, seems affectionate, ruffling her son's hair at one point in the session, making him feel claustrophobic and embarrassed. Several months into treatment, John witnesses a high-school student taunting another outside my office before our session. Visibly shaken, he describes both his identification with the taunted child through recollecting his own experience of being bullied during grammar school as well as his envy of the bully who, it seems to him, cannot be demeaned or humiliated because of his strength. Over many months, we elaborate on his wish to maintain an impervious emotional façade and to strengthen his body so that, in his words, "nobody will ever mess with me again."

Paternal Function in Muscle Dysmorphia

Muscle dysmorphia, which was originally termed "reverse anorexia," has in common with anorexia nervosa that many of those afflicted have also experienced a compromised paternal function. The basic trauma of infancy might be considered the loss of the ideal state of fusion with the mother (Manninen, 1992). This "nursing couple" (Elise, 1998; Winnicott, 1952) is interrupted by a third, someone that competes for the mother's attention. Over time, the developing boy identifies with this third, who is often the father. Through the father's establishing a loving bond with his son, his "attractive function," which also stands for a "nonmother space" (Diamond, 2017, p. 307), fosters the child's capacity to explore the outside world (Abelin, 1971) and facilitates the establishment of his masculine self through the child's identification with his father. For Manninen (1992), the basic condition for the establishment of this form of masculinity is the creation of an emotional barrier against the wish to maintain a dependent relationship with the mother and a corresponding experience of gratification in exploring the outside world.

For patients with muscle dysmorphia, the father, usually largely carrying the paternal function, may not have been able to establish a loving bond with the developing boy and thus foster his separation and individuation and the consolidation of his masculine identity. These patients, in fact, may have experienced their fathers as bigger, stronger, and more expansive and themselves as comparably weak, vulnerable, and shameful. This experience of the paternal function instead threatens the child with the possibility of remaining trapped in symbiosis with the mother, making him feel small, vulnerable, and weak. In the face of this, the child discovers the possibility of idealizing an aspect of the persecutory paternal function, specifically the version of masculinity characterized by "bigness" (Corbett, 2001) and impermeability (Elise, 2001) that it seems to represent. Over time, this splitting leads to increasing idealization of masculine attributes to avoid emotional experiences of weakness, vulnerability, and shame (Brady, 2017). Notably, this conceptualization is consistent with the "masculinity hypothesis" in eating disorders research, which suggests that conformity to masculine gender roles increases the risk for muscularity-oriented body dissatisfaction and disordered eating (Griffiths, Murray, & Touyz, 2015).

This idea has gained some support from empirical research. In a life history examination of 20 males with muscle dysmorphia, a common narrative of childhood victimization through bullying for perceived differences such as being small, weak, or non-athletic emerged. In most cases, the father was identified as the central person involved though in others, sports coaches and peers were mentioned. The men interviewed described how these experiences of relational victimization left them with a heightened awareness of their failings as men and how the obsessive pursuit of muscularity seemed to offer the possibility of consolidating a firmer sense of masculine identity (Tod, Edwards, & Cranswick, 2016). In a recent empirical study, muscle dysmorphia was significantly associated with vulnerable narcissism, which also supports the idea that the self-esteem of these patients has been undermined (Boulter & Sandgren, 2021).

After our work continues to progress, John is increasingly able to speak about his experience with his father who, it seems to him, is invested in maintaining a dominant stance in relation to this son. His stance, we come to believe, might appropriately be described as "bullying": "the exposure of an individual . . . to negative interactions on the part of one or more dominant persons, who gain in some way from the discomfort of their victims" (Twemlow, Sacco, & Williams, 1996, p. 297). His father is likely experiencing himself in these interactions as a good father who is protecting his son, teaching him important lessons, while also defensively shoring up a sense of himself as knowledgeable and powerful in relation to his son, who he experiences as small, vulnerable, and weak. John describes how although he deeply resents his father, he also envies his apparent strength. Bodybuilding, he feels, is a concrete way to develop his own strength so that he will never be bullied and so have an experience of feeling small, vulnerable, and weak again.

References

Abelin, E. L. (1971). The role of the father in the separation-individuation process. In B. McDevitt & C. F. Settlage (Eds.), *Separation-individuation* (pp. 229–252). New York, NY: International Universities Press.

Archer, J. (2004). Sex differences in aggression in real-world settings: A meta-analytic review. *Review of General Psychology, 8*(4), 291–322.

Beresin, E. V., Gordon, C., & Herzog, D. B. (1989). The process of recovering from anorexia nervosa. *Journal of the American Academy of Psychoanalysis and Dynamic Psychiatry, 17*(1), 103–130.

Bers, S. A., Blatt, S. J., & Dolinsky, A. (2004). The sense of self in anorexia-nervosa patients: A psychoanalytically informed method for studying self-representation. *Psychoanalytic Study of the Child, 59*, 294–316.

Bers, S., & Quinlan, D. M. (1992). Perceived-competence deficit in anorexia nervosa. *Journal of Abnormal Psychology, 101*, 423–431.

Boulter, M. W., & Sandgren, S. S. (2021). Me, myself, and my muscles: associations between narcissism and muscle dysmorphia. *Eating Disorders*, 1–7.

Brady, M. (2017). Afflictions related to "ideals" of masculinity: Gremlins within. *Contemporary Psychoanalysis, 53*(2), 196–208.

Bruch, H. (1962). Perceptual and conceptual disturbances in anorexia nervosa. *Psychosomatic Medicine, 24*, 187–194.

Bruch, H. (1973). *Eating disorders: Obesity, anorexia nervosa and the person within*. New York, NY: Basic Books.

Bruch, H. (1978). *The golden cage*. Cambridge, MA: Harvard University Press.

Cafri, G., Thompson, J. K., Ricciardelli, L., McCabe, M., Smolak, L., & Yesalis, C. (2005). Pursuit of the muscular ideal: Physical and psychological consequences and putative risk factors. *Clinical Psychology Review, 25*(2), 215–239.

Cash, T. F., & Pruzinsky, T. (2002). *Body image: A handbook of theory, research & clinical practice*. New York, NY: Guilford Press.

Chasseguet-Smirgel, J. (1993). Troubles alimentaires et feminité: Reflections à partir de cas d'adultes ayant présenté des troubles alimentaires à adolescence [Eating disorders and femininity: Some reflections on adult cases that presented an eating disorder during adolescence]. *Canadian Journal of Psychoanalysis, 1*, 102–122.

Chasseguet-Smirgel, J. (1995). Auto-sadism, eating disorders, and femininity: Based on case studies of adult women who experienced eating disorders as adolescents. In M. A. F. Hanly (Ed.), *Essential papers on masochism*. New York, NY: New York University Press.

Choi, P. Y. L., Pope, H. G., & Olivardia, R. (2002). Muscle dysmorphia: A new syndrome in weightlifters. *British Journal of Sports Medicine, 36*(5), 375–376.

Corbett, K. (2001). Faggot = loser. *Studies in Gender & Sexuality, 2*(1), 3–28.

Davies, N., & Eagle, G. (2013). Conceptualizing the paternal function: Maleness, masculinity, or thirdness? *Contemporary Psychoanalysis, 49*(4), 559–585.

Diamond, M. (2017a). Recovering the father in mind and flesh: History, triadic functioning, and developmental implications. *Psychoanalytic Quarterly, LXXXVI*(2), 297–334.

Diamond, M. (2017b). The missing father function in psychoanalytic theory and technique: The analyst's internal couple and maturing intimacy. *The Psychoanalytic Quarterly*, *86*(4), 861–887.

Dimen, M. (1991). Deconstructing difference: Gender, splitting, and transitional space. *Psychoanalytic Dialogues*, *1*(3), 335–352.

Elise, D. (1998). Gender repertoire: Body, mind, and bisexuality. *Psychoanalytic Dialogues*, *8*(3), 353–371.

Elise, D. (2001). Unlawful entry: Male fears of psychic penetration. *Psychoanalytic Dialogues*, *11*, 499–531.

Elliott, J. C. (2010). Fathers, daughters, and anorexia nervosa. *Perspectives in Psychiatric Care*, *46*, 37–47. https://doi.org/10.1111/j.1744-6163.2009.00236.x

Fiorini, L. G. (2013). Deconstruyendo el concepto de función paterna: un paradigm interpelado [Deconstructing the concept of paternal function]. *Revista de Psicoanálisis*, *70*, 671–682.

Garner, D. M., Garfinkel, P. E., Schwartz, D., & Thompson, M. (1980). Cultural expectations of thinness in women. *Psychological Reports*, *47*, 483–491.

Griffiths, S., Murray, S. B., & Touyz, S. (2015). Extending the masculinity hypothesis: An investigation of gender role conformity, body dissatisfaction, and disordered eating in young heterosexual men. *Psychology of Men & Masculinity*, *16*(1), 108.

Hamburg, P. (1999). The lie: Anorexia and the paternal metaphor. *Psychoanalytic Review*, *86*, 745–769.

Herzog, J. M. (1982). On father hunger: the father's role in the modulation of the aggressive drive and fantasy. In S. H. Cat, A. R. Gurwitt, & J. M. Ross (Eds.), *Father and child: Developmental and clinical perspectives* (pp. 163–174). Boston, MA: Little Brown.

Herzog, J. M. (1988). Preoedipal Oedipus: The father-child dialogue. In G. H. Pollock & J. M. Ross (Eds.), *The Oedipus papers* (pp. 475–491). Madison, CT: International Universities Press.

Herzog, J. M. (2001). *Father hunger: Explorations with adults and children.* Hillsdale, NJ: The Analytic Press.

Herzog, J. M. (2004). Father hunger and narcissistic deformation. *Psychoanalytic Quarterly*, *73*(4), 893–914.

Herzog, J. M. (2010). Fathers and play. *Canadian Journal of Psychoanalysis*, *18*(1), 106–112.

Hildebrandt, T., Schlundt, D., Langenbucher, J., & Chung, T. (2006). Presence of muscle dysmorphia symptomology among male weightlifters. *Comprehensive Psychiatry*, *47*(2), 127–135.

Jacobi, L., & Cash, T. F. (1994). In pursuit of the perfect appearance: Discrepancies among self-ideal percepts of multiple physical attributes 1. *Journal of Applied Social Psychology*, *24*(5), 379–396.

Knox, J. (2011). *Self-agency in psychotherapy: Attachment, autonomy, intimacy*. New York, NY: W.W. Norton & Company.

Lawrence, M. (2001). Body, mother, mind: Anorexia, femininity and the intrusive object. *International Journal of Psychoanalysis, 83*, 837–850.

Maine, M. (1991). *Father hunger: Fathers, daughters, and the pursuit of thinness*. Carlsbad, CA: Gurze Books.

Manninen, V. (1992). The ultimate masculine striving: Reflexions on the psychology of two polar explorers. *Scandinavian Psychoanalytic Review, 15*(1), 1–26.

Novick, J., & Novick, K. (2016). *Freedom to choose: Two systems of self regulation*. New York: International Psychoanalysis Books.

Olivardia, R. (2001). Mirror, mirror on the wall, who's the largest of them all? The features and phenomenology of muscle dysmorphia. *Harvard Review of Psychiatry, 9*(5), 254–259.

Olivardia, R. (2007). Muscle dysmorphia: Characteristics, assessment, and treatment In J. K Thompson & G. Cafri (Eds.), *The muscular ideal psychological, social, and medical perspectives* (pp. 123–139). Washington, DC: American Psychological Association.

Olivardia, R., Pope Jr, H. G., & Hudson, J. I. (2000). Muscle dysmorphia in male weightlifters: A case-control study. *American Journal of Psychiatry, 157*(8), 1291–1296.

Perelberg, J. (2013). Paternal function and thirdness in psychoanalysis and legend: Has the future been foretold? *Psychoanalytic Quarterly, 82*, 557–585.

Ricciardelli, L. A., McCabe, M. P., & Banfield, S. (2000). Body image and body change methods in adolescent boys: Role of parents, friends and the media. *Journal of Psychosomatic Research, 49*(3), 189–197.

Ritvo, S. (1976). Adolescent to woman. *Journal of the American Psychoanalytic Association, 24*, 127–137.

Schoen, S. (2015). "You're the one that I want": Appetite, agency, and the gendered self. In J. Petrucelli (Ed.), *Body-states: Interpersonal and relational perspectives on the treatment of eating disorders* (Psychoanalysis in a New Key). New York, NY: Routledge.

Selvini Palazzoli, M. (1974). *Self-starvation, from individual to family therapy in the treatment of anorexia nervosa* (A. Pomerans, Trans.). Northvale, NJ: Jason Aronson (Original work published 1963).

Sours, J. A. (1974). The anorexia nervosa syndrome. *International Journal of Psychoanalysis, 55*, 567–576.

Tod, D., Edwards, C., & Cranswick, I. (2016). Muscle dysmorphia: Current insights. *Psychology Research and Behavior Management, 9*, 179.

Twemlow, S. W., Sacco, F. C., & Williams, P. (1996). Perspective on the bully-victim-bystander relationship. *Clinic, 60*(31), 296–313.

Winnicott, D. W. (1952). Anxiety associated with insecurity. In *Collected papers: Through paediatrics to psycho-analysis* (pp. 97–100). New York, NY: Basic Books (1975).

Zerbe, K. J. (1993). *The body betrayed: Women, eating disorders, and treatment*. Washington, DC: American Psychiatric Press.

Chapter 9

Eating Disorders in Cyberspace

Introduction

This chapter offers a psychoanalytic perspective on pro-anorexia ("pro-ana") Internet forums. In the form of chat rooms, newsgroups, and websites, pro-anorexia has emerged in recent years as a cultural movement in cyberspace that takes an at least partially positive attitude toward anorexia nervosa and other eating disorders. Notably, there are also "pro-mia" online forums that focus on bulimia nervosa, bodybuilding forums that have many participants who struggle with muscle dysmorphia, as well as a range of other online spaces in which those struggling with food, weight, and shape interact and express themselves. While the online landscape continues to evolve, in this chapter we will focus specifically on pro-anorexia forums both because they have been subjected to the most theoretical and empirical research and because the ideas elaborated here will prove fruitful when thinking about patients who make use of other kinds of online platforms.

The empirical literature documents both the harm and potential benefit pro-anorexia forums offer participants. The deleterious effects of participation, including decreased self-esteem, self-efficacy, and perceived attractiveness, as well as increased negative affect and perception of being overweight, have been clearly demonstrated (Bardone-Cone & Cass, 2007). Recent empirical research, however, takes a nuanced point of view, suggesting that participation has benefits, including social support, a way to cope with a stigmatized illness, and a means of self-expression (Yeshua-Katz

DOI: 10.4324/9781003016991-10

& Martins, 2012). Here we explore how participants make psychological use of these forums. On the one hand, they may provide participants with a potential space (Winnicott, 1971) that fosters psychological development, allowing participants to play with ideas about relationship, identity, and even recovery. For the purposes of this chapter, *potential space* is a state of mind in which play and creativity are possible. In contrast to this, pro-anorexia forums may also provide an opportunity for psychic retreat (Steiner, 1993) in which cyberspace becomes a "funhouse mirror" (Malater, 2007): an escape from a reality that has become unbearable and a place of "relative peace" (Steiner, 1993, p. 1). *Psychic retreats* are problematic because they foreclose the possibility of emotional growth, creativity, and authentic engagement with relationship.

At the outset, it must be acknowledged that while this chapter investigates the constructive psychological use that some participants make of pro-anorexia forums in addition to the harm they may suffer by engaging with them, clinical treatment, especially with adolescents, often involves helping parents think critically about how their children are engaging in cyberspace. At times, this may entail helping parents to set limits with their children that foreclose their participation in these forums entirely. At other times, parents may themselves not yet be psychologically capable of providing or enforcing such limits. Each situation must be evaluated on a case-by-case basis and the ideas developed in this chapter are meant to enhance the clinician's ability to assess the impact that these forums are having on patients.

Pro-Anorexia Forums

Pro-anorexia has emerged in recent years as an Internet-based cultural movement that takes an at least partially positive attitude toward anorexia nervosa and other eating disorders. Most pro-anorexia (commonly referred to as "pro-ana") forums offer guidelines for beginning and maintaining anorexia, tips for rapid weight loss, dieting competitions, ways to avoid detection by family and friends, and motivational images ("thinspiration") to inspire further weight loss (Strife & Rickard, 2011). More than 500 forums exist at a given time, though estimates are unreliable as forums are frequently shut down by their hosts and reopened at new locations (Atkins, 2005; Bardone-Cone &

Cass, 2007). This number vastly exceeds that of recovery-oriented forums (Chesley, Alberts, Klein, & Kreipe, 2003).

The pro-ana community does not reflect a single, coherent philosophy. On the contrary, each site has its own unique perspective of what it means to have an eating disorder – for example, whether eating disorders are a lifestyle or a medical condition (Strife & Rickard, 2011), a positive or negative experience (or both), an experience to be cultivated or to be avoided. In some ways, the pro-ana community is defined in opposition to its adversaries. When an outside user posts an attack on a pro-ana forum or a site is shut down by its host, the resistance of its users and their shared goals and beliefs are strengthened (Giles, 2006)

Like anorexia nervosa itself, pro-ana sites confront visitors with what has been described as "the spectacle of not eating" – words and images conveying profound degrees of emaciation and embodied images of suffering (Warin, 2004). Pro-ana sites have raised intense controversy. Effectively a movement of resistance against conventional conceptualizations and treatments of eating disorders (Giles, 2006), they have raised concern among both health professionals and parents, who express alarm that these forums harm vulnerable individuals (Paquette, 2002). What is the impact of pro-ana forums on participants? The deleterious effects of participation, including decreased self-esteem, self-efficacy, and perceived attractiveness, as well as increased negative affect and perception of being overweight, are documented (Bardone-Cone & Cass, 2007). Recent research, however, takes a nuanced point of view, suggesting that participation has benefits, including social support, a way to cope with a stigmatized illness, and a means of self-expression (Yeshua-Katz & Martins, 2012). Another suggests that participants who sought emotional support on pro-ana forums experienced benefit, whereas those who use the sites for sustaining an eating disorder without seeking emotional support were harmed (Csipke & Horne, 2007).

The fact that pro-ana forums appear to have benefits for some participants is a bracing discovery. Theorists have recently turned their attention to cyberspace, with a growing body of work on the psychological implications of the Internet (Marzi, 2016; Turkle, 1997, 1985), the intersection of psychopathology and cyberspace (Curtis, 2007; Wood, 2011), and the interplay between the Internet and psychoanalysis

(Russell, 2015; Lemma & Caparrotta, 2014; Migone, 2013; Lingiardi, 2008). Without a doubt, cyberspace has introduced a dramatic change into our cultural understanding of reality (Hartman, 2011) but the nature of that change is a matter of ongoing debate. Does cyberspace offer a potential space, an avenue for personal development and growth, or a venue for psychic retreat (Lingiardi, 2008)? In other words, cyberspace has been envisioned as offering an opportunity for creative fantasy and imagination and as a potential "funhouse mirror, trapping the wary and vulnerable in pseudo-reality" (Malater, 2007).

Consider "Sara," a young woman with anorexia nervosa who was first discussed in *Chapter 4: Abjection and Bodily Disgust*. In our work together, we learn that pro-ana forums serve several purposes for her. At times, her participation functions as what Steiner (1993) calls a psychic retreat, a place to withdraw from overwhelming emotional pain. Indeed, in cyberspace she is subject to the same ruminations and fixations and often uses these venues for perseverative thinking separate from relationship. For example, over periods of weeks she recounts posting virtually identical material, often focused on the specifics of calories ingested, calories expended throughout the day, and current body weight. It seems to me this is done not in hope of relational response but as a way of containing her anxieties. These experiences do not contribute to her emotional growth, but rather are a way to make her overwhelming anxiety more manageable.

Over time, particularly as our work progresses, Sara also finds herself able to develop a kind of mutuality (though at a sufficient distance) in her online relationships, which she has not been able to do in the real world. As we explore this, we discover that pro-ana forums provide her with a good enough environment for play: the computer and its connection to cyberspace is sufficiently removed from the exigencies of reality without becoming pure fantasy, a space on the "border between self and not-self" (Turkle, 1997, p. 30). As Gabbard (2001) writes,

> The person sending an e-mail message is alone, but not alone. The apparent privacy allows for freer expression, but the awareness of the other receiving the e-mail allows for passionate attachment and highly emotional expressiveness.

(p. 734)

Pro-ana forums become, at times, a form of potential space for her because they are a move toward relatedness away from purely omnipotent fantasy while retaining an element of control. As Lingiardi (2008) writes, "Spoken dialogue, more than written exchange, seems to confer 'reality' on a phenomenon" (p. 120). She begins to find a way to play with her thoughts and feelings in a space between reality and fantasy, where her fears of traumatic intrusion can be kept at a distance. With this emergence of the capacity to generate potential space, she engages in increasingly imaginative dialogue with her peers. For her, pro-ana forums serve as a space that allows her to imagine different thoughts, feelings, and ways of being in the world without the commitment real-life action entails or with the same level of vulnerability that face-to-face interaction involves. Over time, her emerging capacity for play makes its way into our clinical work. After several years, she relinquishes the forums entirely, in favor of more relational forms of play.

Observations of Pro-Ana Forums

This section draws upon a previously published article (Wooldridge, Mok, & Chiu, 2014) that conducted a qualitative analysis of proanorexia forums. The data gathered supports the thesis that pro-ana forums provide participants with the opportunity to make use of potential space (Winnicott, 1971) for creative play with multiple dimensions of their experience and, at the same time, offer a venue for psychic retreat (Steiner, 1993), an escape from truth and relatedness. In the clinical process, we must assess the ways in which pro-anorexia forums are utilized with respect to each individual patient's underlying psychodynamics at each moment in the treatment.

The architecture of pro-ana forums facilitates the generation of both potential space and psychic retreat. Potential space depends on the capacity to maintain a dialectical process between oneness and separateness, fantasy and reality (Ogden, 1985). For patients with eating disorders, traumatic themes like those discussed in earlier chapters have compromised the capacity to generate potential space. On pro-anorexia forums, the high level of control afforded to participants may allow for certain disturbing aspects of reality to be set aside, making it possible to maintain the dialectical process between fantasy and reality to a degree and for potential space to become temporarily accessible. At other times, reality may become too much to bear and this same control extends into omnipotence, facilitating psychic retreat (Steiner, 1993), in which participants escape from engagement with painful emotional experiences entirely. In this section, we will explore several themes that emerge on these forums with attention to both possibilities.

The experience of alienation is prominent among participants in pro-ana forums. Here young men and women lament their estrangement from friends and family and their extreme loneliness, which is the conscious, affective component of alienation (Burton, 1961). As one participant wrote,

> the nature of the beast being mostly secretive and lonely, it's a comfort to know that others have gone through the same thing. When I first found a similar ED [eating disorder] web site at age 16 I nearly wept with relief – I had suffered alone in silence for almost five years, and didn't know anyone else who had an ED.

Sartre's (1984) elucidation of alienation in his analysis of "the look" assists us in thinking about this aspect of participants' experience. When we are engaged in the immediacy of our lives, we experience the world through a first-person perspective in which others are experienced as objects related to our current pursuits. When we become aware of being looked at – in his words, when our subjectivity is invaded by the subjectivity of another of whose world we are merely a part – we become aware of another, more objective aspect of our nature insofar as it exists as an object in the mind of a separate subjectivity. We become aware that we are alienated from a dimension of our being that resides outside of our immediate experience.

Many participants describe experiencing the other as forcing upon them a disruptively different aspect of reality from their own, subjectively apprehended, experience. They frequently speak about parents and treatment providers who insist that they relinquish their symptoms without an empathic understanding of the underlying struggles that drive their engagement with them. In many cases, this experience of having one's subjectivity invaded by the subjectivity of another reverberates with earlier experiences of traumatic intrusion. In the words of one participant,

Everybody around me thought they knew more about it than I did. I felt like the loneliest person on the planet . . . everyone was telling me what was wrong with me and how I should feel. but its always been that way for me, even before I had the ED my parents never thought me my own person.

Pro-ana forums present participants with the possibility of retreating from the pain inherent in the experience of alienation, for on pro-anorexia forums almost all participants share a remarkable degree of understanding of the underlying pain that drives disordered eating. Of course, psychic retreats can serve as both pathological organizations or as temporary, self-regulatory private spaces that foster resilience and reconsolidation (Steiner, 1993). The problem, in other words, is not the retreat itself but how the retreat is used. When we emerge from retreat, are we more equipped to deal with the exigencies of day-to-day living? As one participant wrote,

When I come on here and talk, I can actually cope, can get through the rest of the day. This place has given me so much strength. Its given me the support I need to get treatment, to reach out to friends.

In this excerpt, a participant makes use of a pro-ana forum as a temporary retreat that allows him to refuel, emerging again into the world of relationship less battered and more resilient than before. Others, however, use pro-ana forums as extended retreats. In the words of one participant, "Why bother with people? They'll fuck you up and disappoint you. Better to stay on the computer." Thus, pro-ana forums can become a way to avoid relational contact that feels too threatening almost entirely. As Faber (1984) has written,

[The computer] offers itself to its manipulator as a powerful little world, a powerful little universe, a kind of microcosm, that can be totally mastered, totally controlled, in such a way as to offset, at the unconscious level, early narcissistic wounds experienced in the failure to master, to control, the primary caregiver or "object."

(p. 267)

At their worst, pro-ana forums serve as a container into which participants evacuate their emotional lives to dissociate from them, engaging in repetitive behaviors that do not lead to emotional growth. The most common of these repetitive behaviors is the declaration of highest weight, current weight, and goal weight. Similarly, participants often repeat their calories eaten or calories burned. These conversations are notable for their lack of involvement with the other; they are posted without expectation of response, and any response that is made is rarely engaged. This is among the most pathological uses of these forums.

While psychic retreat may be helpful for the ego at times, it becomes problematic when used at great length. As participants become increasingly involved with the ethereal world of pro-ana, they may become increasingly detached from the real world, with the physicality (and frailty) it entails. Consider the following excerpt from one participant:

> I spend all my free time here. . . . I dunno what I'd do without all you. Don't really have any friends, nothing worth spending time on. This place has saved me.

Although cyberspace may provide retreat from relational anguish, it also provides the opportunity to make initial steps into a world inhabited by others (Lingiardi, 2008). In some cases, participants make real connections with their peers. The relative safety of cyberspace makes the possibility of relational connection feel within reach for those with fraught histories of emotional intimacy. As one young man wrote,

> Part of why this is the best support site is that people on here are in all stages of [eating] disorders and can come here no matter what they feel about their EDs. I have made real friends here, more than in my RL [real life], where it's so hard.

In this excerpt, we can see a participant who has found "real friends" on a pro-ana site, both because of common experience he shares with other participants and, presumably, because of the kinds of experience an online forum makes possible for him. Indeed, it is because pro-ana sites protect participants against an experience of a reality that is too much to bear that potential space and, thus, deeper relationships become accessible.

Similarly, the atmosphere of tolerance for experimentation and the relational warmth that accompanies many conversations is remarkable. Consider the following excerpt:

> nice to see you here! i think you'll find that people are accepting of what you're going thru. a lot of us are in different stages of recovery and a lot of people are still struggling with their sexual orientation gay? bi? straight? it's a question that i'm always asking myself, still no answers.

There is an implicit agreement within the pro-ana community that the differentiation between "real life" and life in cyberspace will not be confronted. This makes play, which depends heavily on maintaining an illusion of this kind, possible (Winnicott, 1953). When this area of illusion is collapsed by outsiders insisting on the differentiation between real life and life in cyberspace – through "flames," or comments made by hostile site visitors (O'Dochartaigh, 2002), for example – strong responses are elicited (Giles, 2006). Consider the following example of an outsider's critique.

> I know you probably feel you are doing a deed to those who are afflicted with this illness, but the way in which you go about promoting it is not only wrong, it is contributing to the delinquency of others (most of whom are more than likely minors). Giving "diet tips" and encouragement to eat less than the recommended amount of daily calories could be hindering the health of young girls (and perhaps boys) everywhere. It is people like you who continue to put it in these young women's minds that they aren't good enough, when that is simply not true. You think you are the answer, you think you are doing the right thing; you are not. You are the problem with this world.

In this excerpt, we see an outsider's attack on the pro-ana forum, reflecting a collapse of his own ability to understand what the site represents to its participants. Instances such as these are often reacted to with outright aggression; in many cases, moderators remove them from the forum entirely. When the impingement of reality collapses the illusion necessary for play, participants, both as individuals and as a community, make a concentrated effort at the restoration of illusion. The consensus of the pro-ana community and the omnipotence afforded by modern technology are precisely what makes it possible for this illusion to be maintained with relative consistency.

Questions of identity are inherent in pro-ana forums. Among the questions pertaining to identity that are explored on pro-ana forums, perhaps the most common is, "What does it mean to be anorexic?" Pro-ana websites do not reflect a universally coherent standpoint. On the contrary, each site has its own perspective on what it means, and the term 'ana' has become the subject of intense identity negotiation. For example, participants appear to frequently consider whether anorexia is a lifestyle choice or medical condition, a positive experience or a negative one (Giles, 2006).

Individuals with eating disorders find themselves the object of public scrutiny and clinical diagnosis. They must reconcile their own experience of eating disorders as empowering states of distinction with immense symbolic power with the one-sided representation of eating disorders by the media and medical professionals (Warin, 2004). Deprived of their agency, these individuals are likely to seek alternative forums in which they can reclaim their power from outside agencies. Indeed, pro-ana forums provide such a venue, a potential space in which individuals can engage in what has been called "agency play" (Battaglia, 1997, p. 507), which can be seen in the following excerpt:

> I just wanna put it out there that I'm tired of being told what I am by my treatment team. They think they know more than me about what I feel. I'm not a diagnosis; I'm a person who carries around ana by myself all day, every day. And maybe ana is not what they think it is, maybe it's both better and worse.

Here, we can see a participant begin to think about various aspects of her identity and, furthermore, resist having her identity defined primarily by others. In this forum, she can develop a more nuanced perspective about what it means to be "ana" – a perspective that is ultimately more resonant with her experience.

Pro-ana forums also provide a potential space for participants to play with various aspects of identity. As Turkle (1997) argues, the Internet, with its relative anonymity, provides individuals with a laboratory for exploring and experimenting with different versions of self. With the anonymity these forums provide, participants are free to express themselves and behave in ways that are frowned upon in their day-to-day lives (Bargh, McKenna, & Fitzsimmons, 2002). Indeed, in face-to-face interactions, disclosing or experimenting with one's sense of identity can have serious consequences (Derlega, Metts, Petronio, & Margulis, 1993). In contrast, pro-ana forums provide participants with the possibility of inhabiting a space between fantasy and reality; free to fantasize, they are nonetheless in contact with others, but without the same degree of risk found in the real world.

The most striking element of pro-ana forums is visual in nature. In its most common form, "thinspiration" or "thinspo" consists of motivational images of models, actresses, and actors, or even site participants, many of which have been modified to make them appear even more emaciated. Thinspiration image may serve as a concrete representation of a yearning for a particular kind of psychological state: emptied out of toxic projections at the hands of important objects and the capacity to remain impervious to further projections. In many cases, participants develop favorite models as sources of thinspiration, and follow and discuss them over time.

Have you seen the Machinist? I want to look like Bale. he's got no excess at all, totally ripped. If I could look like that, I think id be happy with my life for good – ahhhh contentment.

Often, participants post images of themselves, providing a visual record of their increasing emaciation over time. In these images, we find a visual representation of the participant's internalized object relationship. Lemma (2010) writes that the body can be open and receptive to the other or it can be shut down, keeping the other out. Drawing on Frank (1991), Lemma (2010) describes the *monadic body*, which serves as a psychic retreat (Steiner, 1993), an idealized state that can be used to hold the self together and to resist the regressive pull back into a fused relationship with the mother. Consider the following excerpt:

Im still working on it. No breakfast, coffee only, 3 hours of exercise. Im running seven miles every am. Im going to post some badass thinspo of myself soon! It feels like I barely need food anymore. Its amazing to see!

We might speculate that this participant's "barely needing food" suggests his fight against the allure of dependency. In other cases, thinspiration seems to serve as a kind of communication by impact (Casement, 1991). When I first encountered so-called "thinspiration" images, I felt intruded upon by the intensity of their suffering and frailty. As intrusion and invasion are central to the experience of anorexia nervosa (Williams, 1997), these images seem to say, "I feel invaded by your gaze, and I am going to invade you in return."

Surprisingly, much conversation on pro-ana forums is focused on the possibility of recovery. The experience of eating disorders is fraught with ambivalence (Williams & Reid, 2010). In the literature and in clinical practice, patients report feeling uncertain about whether anorexia is a "friend" or an "enemy" and whether it is a problem that needs treatment (Colton & Pistrang, 2004), often spending a great deal of time weighing its advantages and disadvantages (Cockell, Geller, & Linden, 2003). On these forums, participants find a space in which to play with their ideas about the benefits and risks of their eating disorders. In the following excerpt, a participant gives voice to a "positive" aspect of the anorexic experience.

Have any of the people against ANA been fat? It's the worst feeling. When added to physical problems keeping you from adequate exercise, Ana is a godsend. So I feel really grateful to Ana for that, that she's taken that pain away.

In this excerpt, the participant is commenting on the perceived psychological benefits of anorexia. She experiences her eating disorder as the lesser evil when compared to the feelings of distress she experiences when not actively restricting. In contrast, consider the following post:

I feel unsure, as well. But I don't want to go on starving. Like, I don't want to have an ED, but I don't want to have to eat, either.

In this excerpt, we see a participant with more overtly expressed ambivalence: though eating is a fraught experience, starvation is also understood as a deeply unsatisfying in significant ways as well. In some cases, these forums provide the space for sufferers to play with the idea of recovery in all its dimensions, including weight restoration.

> so what's it like exactly to feel normal weight? I gain a pound and feel fat as all hell so I cant [*sic*] imagine what itd be like to be looking like people I see walking around. but then I look at em and they look happy sometimes, it makes me wonder if its worth it . . . [anorexia]

In this excerpt, a participant is beginning to think about what it might be like to change his relationship to his body and its weight and shape. He is, furthermore, questioning whether the psychological benefits of his disorder justify their cost. In the following excerpt, we encounter a participant who is more motivated toward recovery.

> looking to attempt recovery again, and I'm feeling really fucking passionate about succeeding this time. I'm so done with this chapter of my life, I don't want to restrict and b/p [binge and purge] my brains out all the time. One of the things I've failed to do in the past when attempting recovery is reach out to others doing the same, so I was hoping to find some others on this site who are in whatever stage of recovering just as someone to lean on or even to help encourage. I need all the help I can get!

This participant is strongly motivated to change. He is clearly reaching out for support – an act which may have been made possible through his relationship to pro-ana forums – and has made a connection between receiving emotional support and increasing his chances of recovery.

In each of the themes discussed here – alienation, relational connection and support, questions of identity, and ambivalence about recovery – we see examples of participants making use of pro-anorexia forums to facilitate potential space in which to think creatively, as temporary psychic retreats in which to refuel before further engagement with painful aspects of reality, and as containers into which they evacuate their emotional lives in order to dissociate from them. In fact, the same participants may use the same forums in each of these ways, often in remarkably short spans of time. Ultimately, clinicians are tasked with assessing in each moment how pro-anorexia forums function for each patient and must position themselves appropriately within this shifting landscape of the patient's emotional world as treatment unfolds. In some cases, this may entail working directly with parents to foreclose patients' engagement with these forums entirely. When this is not possible or not immediately warranted, the ideas presented in this chapter may facilitate our efforts to speak with patients in ways that forward their emotional development.

References

Atkins, L. (2005, November 3). It's better to be thin and dead than fat and living. *The Guardian*. Retrieved November 8, 2012, from www.guardian.co.uk/technology/2002/jul/23/lifeandhealth.medicineandhealth

Bardone-Cone, A. M., & Cass, K. M. (2007). What does viewing a pro-anorexia website do? An experimental examination of website exposure and moderating effects. *The International Journal of Eating Disorders*, *40*(6), 537–548.

Bargh, J. A., McKenna, K. Y. A., & Fitzsimmons, G. M. (2002). Can you see the real me? Activation and expression of the "true self" on the internet. *Journal of Social Issues*, *58*(1), 33–48.

Battaglia, D. (1997). Ambiguating agency: The case of Malinowski's ghost. *American Anthropologist*, *99*(3), 505–510.

Burton, A. (1961). On the nature of loneliness. *American Journal of Psychoanalysis*, *21*, 34–39.

Casement, P. (1991). *Learning from the patient*. New York, NY: The Guilford Press.

Chesley, E. B., Alberts, J. D., Klein, J. D., & Kreipe, R. E. (2003). Pro or con? Anorexia nervosa and the internet. *Journal of Adolescent Health*, *32*(2), 123–124.

Cockell, S. J., Geller, J., & Linden, W. (2003). Decisional balance in anorexia nervosa: Capitalizing on ambivalence. *European Eating Disorders Review*, *11*(2), 75–89.

Colton, A., & Pistrang, N. (2004). Adolescents' experiences of inpatient treatment for anorexia nervosa. *European Eating Disorders Review*, *12*(5), 307–316.

Csipke, E., & Horne, O. (2007). Pro-eating disorder websites: users' opinions. *European Eating Disorders Review: The Journal of the Eating Disorders Association, 15*(3), 196–206.

Curtis, A. E. (2007). The claustrum: Sequestration of cyberspace. *Psychoanalytic Review, 94*(1), 99–139.

Derlega, V. L., Metts, S., Petronio, S., & Margulis, S. T. (1993). *Self-disclosure*. London: Sage.

Faber, M. D. (1984). The computer, the technological order, and psychoanalysis: Preliminary remarks. *Psychoanalytic Review, 71*(2), 263–277.

Frank, A. (1991). For a sociology of the body: An analytical review. In N. Featherstone, M. Hepworth, & B. Turner (Eds.), *The body: Social processes and cultural theory*. London: Sage.

Gabbard, G. O. (2001). Cyberpassion: E-rotic transference on the internet. *Psychoanalytic Quarterly, 70*, 719–737.

Giles, D. (2006). Constructing identities in cyberspace: the case of eating disorders. *The British Journal of Social Psychology, 45*(3), 463–477.

Hartman, S. (2011). Reality 2.0: When loss is lost. *Psychoanalytic Dialogues: The International Journal of Relational Perspectives, 21*(4), 468–482.

Lemma, A. (2010). *Under the skin: A psychoanalytic study of body modification*. New York, NY: Routledge.

Lemma, A., & Caparrotta, L. (2014). *Psychoanalysis in the technoculture era*. New York, NY: Routledge.

Lingiardi, V. (2008). Playing with unreality: Transference and computer. *The International Journal of Psychoanalysis, 89*, 111–126.

Malater, E. (2007). Introduction: Special issue on the internet. *The Psychoanalytic Review, 94*, 3–6.

Marzi, A. (Ed.). (2016). *Psychoanalysis, identity, and the internet: Explorations into cyberspace*. London: Karnac Books.

Migone, P. (2013). Psychoanalysis on the internet: A discussion of its theoretical implications for both online and offline therapeutic technique. *Psychoanalytic Psychology, 30*, 291–299.

O'Dochartaigh, N. (2002). *The internet research handbook: A practical guide for students and researchers in the social sciences*. London: Sage Publications.

Ogden, T. (1985). On potential space. *The International Journal of Psychoanalysis, 66*, 129–141.

Paquette, M. (2002). Bad company: Internet sites with dangerous information. *Perspectives in Psychiatric Care, 38*(2), 39–40.

Russell, G. I. (2015). *Screen relations: The limits of computer-mediated psychoanalysis and psychotherapy*. London: Karnac.

Sartre, J. P. (1984). *Being and nothingness. A phenomenological essay on ontology*. New York, NY: Washington Square Press.

Steiner, J. (1993). *Psychic retreats: Pathological organizations in psychotic, neurotic, and borderline patients*. New York, NY: Routledge.

Strife, R. S., & Rickard, K. (2011). The conceptualization of anorexia: The pro-ana perspective. *Journal of Women and Social Work, 26*(2), 213–217.

Turkle, S. (1985). *The second self: Computers and the human spirit*. New York, NY: Simon & Schuster.

Turkle, S. (1997). *Life on the screen: Identity in the age of the internet*. New York, NY: Simon & Schuster.'

Warin, M. (2004). Primitivising anorexia: The irresistible spectacle of not eating. *The Australian Journal of Anthropology, 15*(1), 95–104.

Williams, G. (1997). Reflections on some dynamics of eating disorders: "no entry" defences and foreign bodies. *International Journal of Psychoanalysis, 78*(5), 927–941.

Williams, S., & Reid, M. (2010). Understanding the experience of ambivalence in anorexia nervosa: The maintainer's perspective. *Psychology & Health, 25*(5), 551–567.

Winnicott, D. W. (1953). Transitional objects and transitional phenomena: A study of the first not-me possession. *The International Journal of Psychoanalysis, 34*, 89–97.

Winnicott, D. W. (1971). *Playing and reality*. New York, NY: Basic Books.

Wood, H. (2011). The internet and its role in the escalation of sexually compulsive behaviour. *Psychoanalytic Psychotherapy, 25*(2), 127–142.

Wooldridge, T., Mok, C., & Chiu, S. (2014). A qualitative content analysis of male participation in pro-anorexia forums. *Eating Disorders: Journal of Treatment and Prevention, 22*(2).

Yeshua-Katz, D., & Martins, N. (2012). Communicating stigma: The pro-ana paradox. *Health Communication*, 1–10.

Index